JESUS THE DIVINE PHYSICIAN

"Jesus the Divine Physician"

Copyright ©2023 by Fr James McTavish, FMVD

All rights reserved. No part of this book may be used or reproduced in any manner whatsoever without written permission except in the case of brief quotations embodied in critical articles and reviews.

Front cover shows "Resurrection of Jairus' Daughter" by Vasily Dmitrievich Polenov, 1871. The Museum of the Academy of Arts, St. Petersburg, Russia

Contents

Foreword *by Cardinal "Chito" Tagle, DD*	1
Prologue *by Prof. Terence Kennedy, CSSR*	3
Recommendations	8
Introduction	11
Jesus the Divine Physician	15
Formation of a Catholic Physician	32
Get up Young Man and Live	43
Lazarus, Come Out!	51
Suffering, Death and Eternal Life	61
The Pediatrician as Prophet	78
Decision Making in Neonatal End-of-life Scenarios in Low-income Settings	105
Justice and Health care: When "Ordinary" is Extraordinary	132
"The Lion Roars" - Opposing Euthanasia and Assisted Suicide in the Spirit of Cardinal von Galen	152
How Should My Practice of Medicine Be Different Because of My Catholic Faith?	175
Why the Church Says "Yes" to Life and "No" to IVF	187
Internet Pornography: Some Medical and Spiritual Perspectives	198
Devastating consequences of Sex Trafficking on Women's Health	237
Ministers of Life: A Call to Mission for Healthcare Workers	270
About the Author	302

Foreword by Cardinal "Chito" Tagle, DD

Over ten years ago, I wrote the Foreword for "Choose Life", Fr James' first book on moral issues. I have personally noted the pastoral relevance of Fr McTavish's writings in real life ethical scenarios, and am thus happy again to write a few words for his new book, "Jesus the Divine Physician." As we know, Jesus, the good Doctor, when he saw the crowd lost and helpless, felt compassion and taught them many things (cf. Mark 6:34). His medicine, full of mercy and wisdom, healed the multitudes. This healing mission of our Lord continues in the world today.

In this book, Fr James carefully intertwines insights from Catholic moral theology, his medical experience and the Verbum Dei spirituality to shed light on some contemporary issues in healthcare. Topics covered include the spirituality of medicine, end of life decision making (in both adult and pediatric contexts), and the mission of healthcare workers. The author heeds the exhortations of Vatican II to make the presentation of moral theology more scientific in nature, nourished more with the Word of God, and directed towards the vocation of the lay faithful to bear much fruit (cf. *Optatam Totius*, n. 16). Bearing in mind that theological refection is "fruitful only if it is done with an open mind and on one's knees" (Pope Francis), the author combines ethics and spirituality to also broach challenging pastoral issues such as prostitution & human trafficking, and the pandemic of internet pornography.

JESUS THE DIVINE PHYSICIAN

The content of the essays aims to be faithful to the missionary exhortation of Pope Francis that "proclaiming the Gospel message to different cultures also involves proclaiming it to professional, scientific and academic circles. This means an encounter between faith, reason and the sciences" (*Evangelii Gaudium*, n. 132). The concluding essay on "Ministers of Life" reminds us, especially healthcare workers, of the vital mission we have to allow Jesus, the Divine Physician, to continue his healing and saving work through each and every one of us.

I thank Fr. McTavish for making this precious work, which blends solid research with pastoral sensitivity, available to a wide audience.

May the Lord continue to bless his ministry.

Cardinal Luis Antonio "Chito" Tagle, DD

Pro-Prefect for the Section of Evangelization, Dicastery for Evangelization

Prologue by Prof. Terence Kennedy, CSsR

What has fundamental moral theology got to do with bioethics? Why would an expert in bioethics invite a moral theologian to introduce his *Jesus the Divine Physician*? My surprise and joy could not have been greater than when I received an e-mail from Father James with that request.

My mind flew back to when he was a student of moral theology in the Accademia Alfonsiana in Rome 2007-2008. As a candidate for the Licence, he was required to write a thesis, a *tesina*. Born in Scotland, he joined and became a priest in a new religious order from Spain, the *Verbum Dei* missionaries, whom he met in Sydney. They introduced him to their way of living God's Word in the Sacred Scriptures. He was then in his late twenties and dedicated in his profession as a trainee plastic surgeon.

Besides my competence in moral theology, he recognized in me a Redemptorist who had preached parish missions and therefor knew the art of rhetoric not just in theory but had learnt what it could do in practice. He was motivated by the fact that he possessed a mountain of medical knowledge that he wanted to get it through to the faithful. But so much of it was outside their grasp or comprehension. His purpose was to be popular in the sense of reaching the widest possible audience to make available the best that medical research could provide. No mean task that very few manage to pull off!

He aspired also to be expert in a field that marries science with communication. He aimed to lift communication up to another level by seeing bioethics through the eyes of faith. Now faith means having a personal direct relationship with Christ. His book is full of spirituality that inspired a plastic surgeon to see what he could do "to heal the Body of Christ" as a priest.

He ministered for eighteen years in the Philippines, citing many examples of dire poverty, of how people are deprived of the most basic health care simply taken for granted in developed counties. He pleads their cause with the doctors and nurses who have abandoned their country for greener pastures in wealthy nations. He always pays close attention to the practices and standards of the medical profession. The reader can learn much from him about internet pornography and the devastating consequences of sex trafficking in third world countries. He puts forward practical remedies for these horrid and morally disturbing situations.

His determination about the project of his *tesina* impressed me. He was serious about getting to grips with rhetoric's classical tradition, something still influential in contemporary communication theory. He became familiar with that tradition by wading through works by Aristotle and Cicero, authors who form and mold the discipline even today. However, he also chose Quintilian, the heir to their wisdom who became the master of persuasion by expanding rhetoric in new directions in original ways.

Prologue

Acknowledged as the schoolmaster of Europe he showed educators how to pass on culture's treasures from one generation to the next. A pagan, his methods were assimilated into the Christian tradition. Fathers of the Church like Augustine and John Chrysostom were all well versed in the art of classical rhetoric. St. Alphonsus followed in his *Selva di materia praedicabili*, which is a model for Father McTavish's efforts.

Perhaps his project involved more extensive reading than anticipated. In recompense Fr James gained firsthand knowledge of Quintilian's *Institutio Oratoria*'s many dimensions. The three sources of persuasion, *logos*, *pathos*, and *ethos* provide a key to McTavish's approach in his *tesina* on "Persuasion through Character in Ancient Rhetoric".

Rhetoric, the art that conceals art, often leaves us quite unaware of how it weaves its magic, while we delight in its fruits. *Logos* is evident in his expert knowledge of medicine; in the anthropology and social sciences he uses to understand the cultures where he labored. But his chief source is not just *logos* but *the* Logos, Christ himself, the light that enlightens every person that comes into existence. Father McTavish's attitude to *pathos* is to spread Christ's compassion to every person he encountered, to became an instrument of Christ's passion for the weak and downtrodden of whatever social condition.

Ethos seems the most difficult quality to assess. We might ask how does rhetoric fit into ethics. A much-repeated insight from Alasdair MacIntyre helps us here.

JESUS THE DIVINE PHYSICIAN

Aristotle's ethical teaching draws on three founts, the Ethics, Politics and Rhetoric. Rhetoric is an intrinsically ethical venture that brings the *ars dicendi* as technique under sound moral criteria. Beyond abstract standards, the strongest motive for accepting anything as persuasive is its author's character. No matter of mere mechanical technique it is deeply and truly human as St. Augustine demonstrates in Book 4 of his *De Doctrina Christiana*. Where did Father McTavish find this personal criterion enfleshed and put into practice? It is all in the book's title, Jesus the Divine Physician.

Of course, flashes of humor "make the medicine go down". Like when a young woman landed back in the plastic surgeons' care just two weeks after an operation. She had gone to the bowling alley. But as she bowled, she could not get her tiny hand free and hit herself on the head. Back to hospital into the hands of her old friends the plastic surgeons. They fixed her up again and left her to rest. Not five minutes had gone by when the monitors registered flat, absolutely flat. No activity whatsoever! The surgeon rushed back. He found her sitting bolt upright in bed glaring intently at the monitor. "Doctor, am I dead?' she squeaked. He just glanced around. "No! You've just knocked the connection off your chest!"

This episode illustrates Chaïm Perelman's contention that the main *topos* in contemporary rhetoric is presence. The capacity to make a truth, a fact, an event or a story actually present to an audience makes communication effective.

Prologue

It is now time to leave rhetoric behind and let readers discover Father James McTavish's wit and wisdom for themselves. Or, in the *augurio* that the Italians love: "Buona fortuna e buona lettura!" (Good luck and good reading!)

Terence Kennedy, C.Ss.R.
Emeritus Professor, Accademia Alfonsiana, Rome.

JESUS THE DIVINE PHYSICIAN

Recommendations

"In Jesus the Divine Physician, Fr. James McTavish has compiled 14 outstanding award-winning essays in medical ethics from a faith-based perspective. They address a broad range of urgent and ethically challenging questions arising in health care that Catholic and other faith-based healthcare professionals need to address in an ethically sound way to continue and advance the healing and saving mission of Christ in health care today." *William F. Sullivan, MD, CCFP, PhD (Philosophy), Professor of Family Medicine, Georgetown University School of Medicine / Joseph P. Kennedy Sr. Chair in Bioethics, Kennedy Institute of Ethics / Senior Scholar, Kennedy Institute of Ethics, Georgetown University / Ordinary Member, Pontifical Academy for Life*

"An engaging series of essays on topics of great contemporary interest. His discussions addressing the way that the life of faith impacts the ministry of health care workers and the paramount importance of an intense spiritual life and solid spiritual formation for physicians and nurses are eminently helpful." *Father Tad Pacholczyk, Ph.D., The National Catholic Bioethics Center, Philadelphia, USA*

"'Jesus, the Divine Physician' is a thoughtful, provocative and impassioned examination of Catholic teaching on medicine and medical ethics. Fr McTavish draws on his personal experience as a doctor and as a

Prologue

missionary, sharing anecdotes that are sometimes amusing, and self-deprecating, other times deeply moving and powerful. He challenges the reader to consider their conscience, their faith and their attitudes to sickness, mortality and brotherly love." *Professor Dominic Wilkinson, Professor of Medical Ethics, University of Oxford*

"Fr. James McTavish brings his extensive experience as a physician, a theologian, and a pastor working for many years in the Philippines and other countries to reflect upon the vocational call of health care workers and pressing moral issues in health care. Attentive readers will find this book equally inspiring, challenging, and thought-provoking." *Jason T. Eberl, Ph.D., Professor of Health Care Ethics and Philosophy & Director, Albert Gnaegi Center for Health Care Ethics, Saint Louis University, Missouri, USA*

"Fr McTavish brings the light of faith to his medical training and clinical encounters. His habit of thoughtful reflection on his experiences makes these essays worthy of careful reading.

They are fruits of a Catholic faith and professional commitment in different clinical settings - an emergency room or an intensive care ward in an affluent country, the tenement home of a poor family in a low-income setting." *Dr Bernadette Tobin, Director, Plunkett Centre for Ethics, Australian Catholic University*

"I am sure that for those of us dedicated to evangelization, reading his essays motivates us to respond with seriousness and dedication to the questions that we frequently find ourselves confronted by in different areas of our missionary work. 'Jesus, the Divine Physician' is a book that offers great insights to help men and women of good will who work in the health area, opening up possibilities for reflection and guidance for an assertive response to human suffering and pain. *Alfonso Martinez Luna, General responsible (with his wife Adriana) of the Verbum Dei Missionary Couples, Bachelor of Theology and Medical Doctor*

"Fr James McTavish's reflections are incredibly accessible, and highlight Catholic practical wisdom from the heart of Jesus in the midst of the Church's mission. Ethicists, doctors and nurses, and anyone wrestling with life and death issues of any kind will learn much, feel inspired and be challenged to step up to the need at hand. As he writes, if you don't have a mission, find one. Highly recommended!" *Dr Nigel Zimmerman, Adjunct Senior Lecturer, University of Notre Dame Australia*

"An excellent spiritual guide for Catholics in healthcare" *Dr Pravin Thevathasan, Consultant Psychiatrist, Editor, Catholic Medical Quarterly, UK*

"I highly recommend this book as a reference and treasure for anyone called to care for the sick" *Dr. Resti Ma. M. Bautista, Neonatologist*

Introduction

This book contains various essays on the topics of health, healing, suffering, sickness, death and eternal life. It considers the role of faith and the medical mission of Christ, who as the Divine Physician, came to bring us healing and salvation. Through the medicine of his love and mercy, he wanted to save us and give us life to the full (see John 10:10). The questions surrounding health are challenging. The *Catechism* explains, "illness and suffering have always been among the gravest problems confronted in human life. In illness, man experiences his powerlessness, his limitations, and his finitude. Every illness can make us glimpse death" (Catechism of the Catholic Church 1997, n. 1500). Why sickness and suffering? Do they have any meaning? What to do when a loved one is sick? What is the role of our faith in healing? What happens when we die? This book hopes to shed some light on these areas.

Most of the essays were initially given as talks and formations, usually in the hospital or medical school setting, to those involved in healthcare, aware that "proclaiming the Gospel message to different cultures also involves proclaiming it to professional, scientific and academic circles" (*Evangelii Gaudium*, n. 132). As we are faithful to our mission of evangelization, we receive more understanding. Pope Francis explains "the work of evangelization enriches the mind and the heart; it opens up spiritual horizons; it makes us more and more sensitive to the workings of the Holy Spirit" (*Evangelii Gaudium*, n. 272).

JESUS THE DIVINE PHYSICIAN

The first essay, entitled "Jesus the Divine Physician," won 1st place for best essay in the Scholarly magazines category of the 2019 Catholic Press Association (CPA) awards of the United States and Canada. All glory and honor are yours Almighty Father!

"Formation of a Catholic Physician" considers the essential elements in the formation of Catholic doctors. "Get up Young man and Live," (Honorable Mention, Catholic Press Association Awards 2012, Best Essay, Special Interest Newsletter) relates my personal testimony of passing from a plastic and reconstructive surgeon, to becoming a Verbum Dei missionary priest dedicated to the evangelization. "Lazarus, Come Out!" shows the challenge of health care in resource limited settings, and the vitality of faith. "Suffering, Death and Eternal Life" explores key themes at the end of life and beyond.

"The Pediatrician as Prophet" (Third Place, Catholic Press Association Awards 2021, Best Essay - Scholarly Magazines) outlines the specific mission of pediatric doctors. Decisions regarding medical care become difficult when the patient is a seriously ill newborn baby and this issue is discussed in "Decision Making in Neonatal End-of-life Scenarios in Low-income Settings." "Justice and Health care: when 'Ordinary' is Extraordinary" explains Church teaching on end-of-life issues when resources are scarce in the developing world context. In "The Lion Roars - Opposing Euthanasia and Assisted Suicide in the Spirit of Cardinal von Galen" the life and preaching of Cardinal von Galen, and his courageous stance against the

Introduction

euthanasia program of the Nazis in World War II, is outlined. The essay "How Should My Practice of Medicine Be Different Because of My Catholic Faith?" (Second Place, Catholic Press Association Awards 2020, Best Feature Article: Scholarly Magazine) gives practical advice for Catholic healthcare Workers (CHW). "Why the Church Says "Yes" to Life and "No" to IVF" explains the Magisterial teaching on In Vitro Fertilization (IVF).

The healing that Christ brings touches all areas of our humanity, including our wounded sexuality. "Internet Pornography: Some Medical and Spiritual Perspectives" (Third Place, Catholic Press Awards 2021, Best Guest Column/Commentary) explores the pornography pandemic and its consequences. "Devastating consequences of sex trafficking on women's health" (Second Place, Catholic Press Association Awards 2018, Best Feature Article: Scholarly Magazine) explains Church teaching regarding prostitution and sex trafficking as well as their medical and moral implications. The final essay is "Ministers of Life: A Call to Mission for Healthcare Workers." May each healthcare worker respond enthusiastically to the call to mission: "Here I am Lord, send me!" (Isaiah 6:8). It is hoped through the various essays that the reader may understand more fully the healing and saving mission of Jesus, the good Doctor, and in this way, to understand the call to participate in the healing mission of Christ today.

Fr James McTavish, FMVD

1 December 2023

JESUS THE DIVINE PHYSICIAN

> Won 1st place for best essay in the Scholarly magazines category of the 2019 Catholic Press Association (CPA) awards of the United States and Canada

Summary

During his earthly life, Jesus was very active in his ministry of healing. He cured the blind, opened the ears of the deaf, and brought the dead back to life. The early Church Fathers gave our Lord the title of "the Divine Physician." However, Jesus did not cure all disease and sickness once and for all. Instead, he asked us to have faith, to renounce sin, with its concomitant morbidity and mortality, and to believe in him. Jesus came to give us a life that will never end, not even with death. The Church and her members have the ongoing task of continuing his healing work in the world of today.

I was asked to give a talk at the "Forum for Breast Cancer," held at Makati Medical Center, Manila, Philippines. Participants included healthcare workers as well as breast cancer patients, survivors, and their relatives and friends. I focused on various aspects of Christ as the Divine Physician and posed various interactive questions to the audience: what did the healing work of Jesus consist of? What is the role of faith in healing? Is it wrong to desire good health? How to live with sickness? Is there a connection between sin and sickness? What reasons can maintain our hope? Jesus exercised the ministry of healing, and the gospels are littered with examples of him curing the sick: "At sunset, all who had people sick with various diseases brought them to him. He laid his hands on each of them and cured them" (Lk 4:40). As for specialties, we could say his healing work encompassed ophthalmology (opening the eyes of the blind), ENT - ear, nose and throat (curing the deaf), dermatology (healing leprosy), rehabilitation (curing paralysis), hand surgery (healing a withered hand), plastics and reconstruction (repairing a severed ear), neurology (treating a boy with convulsions), critical care (saving the slave of a centurion who was about to die), to name but a few. In his preaching, Jesus refers twice to doctors: "Those who are well do not need a physician, but the sick do" (Mt 9:12), and "Surely you will quote me this proverb, 'Physician, cure yourself'" (Lk 4:23).

Faith-Related Healing

The healing episodes were often related to the faith of the person, and at times Jesus could not do great healings because of a lack of faith of the people (see Mk 6:5).

Why was Jesus interested in the faith of the people? Why not just cure everyone and wipe out disease and sickness once and for all? Surely this is what a compassionate God would do? Our questions arise from a desire to live. Jesus comes precisely to fulfill that desire and tells us so. "A thief comes only to steal and slaughter and destroy; I came so that they might have life and have it more abundantly" (Jn 10:10). This abundant life is not one that only lasts seventy years or eighty if we are strong (see Ps 90:10), but it is eternal life.

Health and Salvation

How can we deepen our understanding of the need for faith in the healings of Jesus? Pope Benedict XVI explained it well in an Angelus address on the healing of the ten lepers.

> This Sunday's Gospel presents Jesus healing ten lepers, of whom only one, a Samaritan and therefore a foreigner, returned to thank him (see Lk 17:11-19). The Lord said to him: "Rise and go your way; your faith has made you well" (Lk 17:19). This Gospel passage invites us to a twofold reflection. It first evokes two levels of healing: one, more superficial, concerns the body. The other deeper level touches the innermost depths of the person, what the Bible calls "the heart", and from there spreads to the whole of a person's life. (Benedict XVI 2007)

I remember during my plastics and reconstructive surgery fellowship training in Sydney, Australia, I saw a young man who slashed his wrist with a desire to commit suicide. After a long operation to reconstruct various tendons and nerves I visited the boy the next morning. I told the boy that we had fixed his hand. He started to cry. I asked him "Why are you crying? The worst part is over. We fixed your hand." He replied "You fixed my hand but who is going to fix my life?"

The young man I saw was in "good" health but he lacked the essential - the desire to live.[1] An operation can cure the superficial wounds, but to heal the deeper wounds, surely the help and grace of Jesus the Good Doctor is needed. Pope Benedict XVI explains further:

> Complete and radical healing is "salvation." By making a distinction between "health" and "salvation", even ordinary language helps us to understand that salvation is far more than health: indeed, it is new, full and definitive life. Furthermore, Jesus here, as in other circumstances, says the words: "Your faith has made you whole." It is faith that saves human beings, re-establishing them in their profound relationship with God, themselves and others; and faith is expressed in gratitude. (Benedict XVI 2007)

Sickness or Health? Ask the Saints

For sure, physical health is a great good and to be desired. Some saints were very sick and prayed for God's intercession to heal them. St Teresa of Ávila suffered terribly and, in her autobiography, writes:

> So strong were the medicines that after two months I was almost dead, ... I was in such agony that they feared I might go mad.... That night I had an attack which left me insensible for almost four days. They gave me the

Jesus the Divine Physician

Sacrament of Extreme Unction, and in every minute of every hour thought that I was dying. They never stopped reciting the Creed to me, as though I could have heard what was said. At times they were so sure that I was dead that afterwards I actually found some wax on my eyelids.... For a day and a half, a grave was left open in my convent, waiting for my body; and the rites for the dead were performed at a friary of our Order a short distance away.... When I saw myself so paralyzed and still so young, and how the physicians of the world had dealt with me, I decided to invoke those of heaven to heal me. For though I bore my illness most joyfully, I still wanted to get well. But sometimes I reflected that I might regain my health and yet be lost, and that it would be better to stay as I was. But I always thought that I should serve God much better if I recovered. This is our mistake, never to resign ourselves absolutely to what the Lord does, though He knows best what suits us.... I took as my lord and advocate the glorious St. Joseph, commending myself earnestly to him. (Teresa of Ávila 1957, 42-6)

St. Alphonsus Liguori, the patron of moral theology in the Catholic Church, discusses sickness in his treatise of 1755 called *Uniformity with God's Will*. Let us consider his wise counsel regarding sickness and health.

- "We ought to make use of the ordinary remedies in time of sickness - such is God's will" (Liguori 1952, n. 4). Here he advises that we

should do all in our power to help and heal ourselves.
- "It is not wrong to ... ask God to free us from our sufferings" (Liguori 1952, n. 4).
- Sometimes we desire health not for love of God but for love of self. "When we find ourselves confined to our sickbed, let us utter this one prayer: "Thy will be done."
- Let us repeat it time and time again and it will please God more than all our mortifications and devotions. There is no better way to serve God than cheerfully to embrace his holy will" (Liguori 1952, n. 4).
- St. Alphonsus cites an example of a person, who prayed for a cure and when healed asked, "Suppose it would be better for my soul's salvation if I remained sick, what point then is there in being well?" (Liguori 1952, n. 4). The sickness returned, and the man was happy to accept the will of God.
- "However, if we decide to ask for health, let us do so at least always resigned and with the proviso that our bodily health may be conducive to the health of our soul" (Liguori 1952, n. 4).

Looking at the life and teachings of these two saints, Teresa of Ávila and Alphonsus Liguori, we know that health is a gift but is subordinate to the higher gift of salvation. Good health can be desired and asked for, but if we remain sick, despite doing our part and following the medical advice, we should resign ourselves to do the will of God.

The book of Sirach summarizes this advice nicely: "My son, when you are ill, do not delay, but pray to God, for it is he who heals. ... Then give the doctor his place lest he leave; you need him too, for there are times when recovery is in his hands. He too prays to God that his diagnosis may be correct and his treatment bring about a cure. Whoever is a sinner before his Maker will be defiant toward the doctor" (Sir 38: 9, 13-15).

I like to remind the other priests in my community of this verse especially when they seem to be ignoring my medical advice!

Can Sin Cause Sickness?

A common understanding in biblical times was that a person was sick because of sin. Some biblical accounts in the New Testament blame sickness on demons. How can we interpret or understand this today?

We Should Take Care Not to Attribute All Sickness to Sin

In one biblical episode, Jesus and his disciples came across a man blind from birth. The disciples ask Jesus "Rabbi, who sinned, this man or his parents, that he was born blind?" Jesus answered, "Neither he nor his parents sinned; it is so that the works of God might be made visible through him" (see Jn 9:1-3).

More troubling for us today perhaps is to see how often sickness in biblical times was attributed to

JESUS THE DIVINE PHYSICIAN

demons. The Gospels are scattered with episodes of Jesus healing the sick by casting out their demons. In Matthew's gospel alone, demons were blamed for muteness (see Mt 9:32), blindness (see Mt 12:22), and what was probable epilepsy (see Mt 17:15). Care should be taken not to directly transpose our current understanding of demons, and medicine, to these episodes.

Once I went to consult an orthopedic spine surgeon regarding repeated episodes of back pain which had caused me various troubles accompanied with much anxiety. The brother of the surgeon happened to be a priest, and also the chief exorcist of the Archdiocese of Manila. Following the consultation and the wise words of the spine surgeon, my anxiety dissipated, and I felt a deep peace. Slightly tongue in cheek, I said to the surgeon "So, it seems like you also have the gift of exorcism and the ability to cast out demons." He looked at me slightly surprised and replied "Why do you say that? That is my older brother. He is the exorcist." "Well," I continued, "when I came into your office, I was plagued by the demon of anxiety, with much concern as to the unpredictability of my back pain and my lack of insight into its cause. However, having listened to your advice, I now feel much peace, as if the demon of anxiety has been expelled." We both laughed as I told him "So I see it is not only your brother priest who has the gift of expelling demons but you too!"

"Sin" May Contribute to or Cause Sickness

The emergency room on Fridays and Saturdays in the United Kingdom is quasi full of people who are intoxicated with alcohol (which incidentally is also known as "the demon drink"!) They present having fought or fallen or having had a motor vehicle accident, among other causes. Most of the doctors, nurses, and healthcare personnel, having seen so many casualties could testify to the "sinfulness" of alcohol abuse and its effects, as well as the exorbitant cost to the hospital and healthcare system of treating alcohol-induced trauma and sickness. No immediate judgment is implied on the persons who have drunk, but it is also important to name things as they are. We might be inclined to agree with the Psalmist who pronounced that they became sick because of their sins (see Ps 107:17).

Various sicknesses and illnesses may have a sinful root or cause. One of the biggest health issues in the United States today is obesity. There can be various medical solutions proposed. One causative factor should not be ignored: gluttony. This word is rarely mentioned in both medical (and spiritual circles.) Screwtape, the senior demon, in his letter to his nephew Wormwood, a junior tempter astutely writes "My dear wormwood, the contemptuous way in which you spoke of gluttony as a means of catching souls, in your last letter, only shows your ignorance. One of the great achievements of the last hundred years has been to deaden the human conscience on that subject, so that by now you will hardly find a sermon preached or a conscience troubled about it in the whole length and breadth of Europe" (Lewis 1961, 86).

In the Philippines, there are forty-seven newly diagnosed cases of HIV every day. Of these, forty-two occur in males who have sex with other males. The sin of lust surely contributes in some way to the high rates of HIV in this group. Other examples could be given but suffice to say that sin has its own morbidity and mortality.[2]

We will now consider sin at societal level and see how it significantly contributes to sickness. By way of many smaller personal sins, and sins of omission, many societies do not have the healthcare they should have.

The Sin of Lack of Healthcare

Pope Francis noted that "at times families suffer terribly when, faced with the illness of a loved one, they lack access to adequate health care" (Francis 2016, n. 44). The lack of accessible healthcare should be a concern for us all. Sometimes it does not bother us as much as it should. It could be a form of "numbing of conscience" (Francis 2015a, n. 49), and thus there is a call "to reawaken our conscience, too often grown dull in the face of poverty" (Francis 2015b, n. 15).

I remember meeting a poor man who had a huge facial mass, most likely cancer. He was living in total misery. I went to visit him with some nuns and children to sing Christmas carols and try to bring some joy in the middle of darkness. After the visit, I was invited to a lovely house in a wealthy suburb for what seemed like a banquet. My seatmate at table, a "good" Catholic and regular mass goer, shared how his dog had become sick recently and how he strived to give it the best veterinary care possible even if it had cost a fortune. I could bear it no longer! I launched into an impassioned speech about the lack of healthcare for the poor and how it should challenge us that many poodles got better healthcare than people. I felt so bad after, and I think I gave the poor man indigestion.

Later, after the sumptuous chocolate mousse dessert, the man approached me. "Father," he said "you really provoked my conscience. It is true what you said, and we need to be reminded of the plight of our poor brothers and sisters." He gave me $200 for the MRI scan that was needed. It made me think that we each have a duty, as part of our Christian prophetic mission, to speak out even if at times it can cause indigestion in us and in our listeners.[3]

Exacerbated by Corruption

One Filipino senator, Alan Peter Cayetano, stated that 6 out of 10 Filipinos die without seeing a doctor and many public hospitals lack equipment and medicines. He linked this situation with corruption: "By cleansing the government of corruption, we will be able to provide our people better and more social services and programs like universal healthcare coverage" (Frialde 2016). Pope Francis had some strong words for those involved in corruption stating that it is a "festering wound," "a grave sin," "an evil," "a sinful hardening of the heart," and "a work of darkness" (Francis 2016, n. 19).

JESUS THE DIVINE PHYSICIAN

Structural Sins

Corruption can mean that dedicated government funds never reach the intended hospital or clinic. Instead, the money is siphoned off before it arrives. Hospital emergency departments will say they have no budget for necessary medicines, and local clinics cannot offer basic services like disease screening; and all because the allocated funds never arrived. Pope John Paul II wrote that "one cannot easily gain a profound understanding of the reality that confronts us unless we give a name to the root of the evils which afflict us" (John Paul II 1987, n. 36).

The name given by Catholic social teaching to such a situation of lack of healthcare is a "structure of sin." Situations of sin are always rooted in many personal sins as Pope John Paul II explained.

> Whenever the Church speaks of situations of sin, or when she condemns as social sins certain situations or the collective behavior of certain social groups, big or small, or even of whole nations and blocs of nations, she knows and she proclaims that such cases of social sin are the result of the accumulation and concentration of many personal sins. It is a case of the very personal sins of those who cause or support evil or who exploit it; of those who are in a position to avoid, eliminate or at least limit certain social evils but who fail to do so out of laziness, fear or the conspiracy of silence, through secret complicity or indifference; of those who take refuge in the supposed impossibility of changing

the world, and also of those who sidestep the effort and sacrifice required, producing specious reasons of a higher order. The real responsibility, then, lies with individuals. A situation - or likewise an institution, a structure, society itself - is not in itself the subject of moral acts. (John Paul II 1984, n. 16)

Reasons to Hope

I wrap up with some strong reasons to hope in the power of Jesus as Divine Physician and the importance of our collaboration.

We are co-workers

The challenges of health care are great and at times can feel overwhelming, especially when trying to counter the deleterious effects on health care of structural sin. Pope Francis cautions us "the battle against evil is a long and hard one; it requires patience and endurance" (Francis 2013).

We should remember that it is Christ's mission and not ours. We are not the Messiah! He is the Good Doctor - we are just his assistants and should try not to get in the way too much. "We are God's co-workers" (1 Cor 3:9) as St Paul reminds us.

Give life to the body

When someone arrives at the emergency room badly injured from multiple gunshot wounds for example, medical personnel have to get access to the veins. Once they get access to the body, they can give fluids, blood, and all the medicines needed. Rev. Jaime Bonet shared that as the injection in the vein of the arm strengthens the entire body, just so the life that passes through only one soul heals the whole Church (see Bonet 1999, 544).

How much good can pass through one docile soul! This should give us reasons to hope. This is a beautiful and encouraging analogy for all of us! Our Lord can give so much life through a healthcare worker who remains united to him (see Jn 15:4-5).

All shall be well

Where the situation seems beyond us, we do well to remember the reassuring words that our Lord addressed to Dame Julian of Norwich - "All shall be well."[4] When we see wounded realities around us in the body of Christ, we should always remember to ask Jesus, the Head, what he wants for his body. After all he is the Good Doctor and has the remedy - the medicine of his love for all the ailments in his body.[5]

Christ himself gives value to each and every act of kindness and goodness done to a patient. After all he is present in each one of them as he explained saying "I was ill and you cared for me" (see Mt 25:36).

Continuing his mission

Jesus the Divine Physician desires to continue his same mission of healing in the world of today. The *Catechism* explains "The Lord Jesus Christ, physician of our souls and bodies, who forgave the sins of the paralytic and restored him to bodily health, has willed that his Church continue, in the power of the Holy

Spirit, his work of healing and salvation, even among her own members" (Catechism 1997, n. 1421).

Our Lord wants to continue stretching out his healing hands to touch, bless and cure the sick. In fact, the etymology of the word "surgeon" is "one who works with his or her hands." We are his healing hands, as the song attributed to the prayer of St Teresa of Ávila reminds us: "Christ has no hands on earth but yours." We can all continue to reach out a helping hand to cure the spiritual and moral ailments of our brothers and sisters. In this way, we continue to assist Jesus, the Divine Physician, in his ongoing mission of healing and giving life to the world of today.

Notes

1. This paradox is also sadly noted in countries such as Japan, with technologically advanced healthcare systems but consistently high suicide rates. In 2015, around 24,000 Japanese people took their own lives; the first time in 18 years that the number of suicides fell below 25,000 (Japan Today 2016).

2. An interesting exercise would be to take the seven deadly sins in turn (pride, anger, lust, envy, greed, gluttony, and laziness) and see in what way each contributes and/or causes sickness and illness. Perhaps this could be the inspiration for a future article.

3. Rev. Jaime Bonet, the founder of the *Fraternidad Misionera Verbum Dei* community, has been known to advise young missionaries in formation to beware of

speakers and speeches that only produce in the audience a "Wow!" of amazement and never an "Ow!" of *metanoia* and change.

4. The Catholic Church recognizes the wisdom of Mother Julian of Norwich, quoting her writings in its *Catechism* (see *Catechism* 1997, n. 313).

5. St Ignatius of Antioch, in his letter to the Church of Ephesus, wrote that the Eucharist is the medicine of immortality.

References

Benedict XVI, Pope. 2007. *Angelus*, St. Peter's Square, Sunday, October 14.

Catechism of the Catholic Church. 1997. 2nd ed. Vatican City: Libreria Editrice Vaticana.

Bonet, Jaime. 1999. *Familiares de Dios, Spiritual exercises for married couples*. Palma de Mallorca, Spain: Fundación Barceló.

Francis, Pope. 2013. *Angelus*. Saint Peter's Square, October 20.

Francis, Pope. 2015a. *Laudato Si'*.

Francis, Pope. 2015b. *Misericordiae Vultus*.

Francis, Pope. 2016. *Amoris Laetitia*.

Frialde, Mike. 2016. Cayetano vows to end corruption in country's healthcare sector. *The Philippine Star*, March 8.

Japan Today. 2016. Number of suicides in Japan drops below 25,000 for first time in 18 years.

John Paul II, Pope. 1984. *Reconciliatio et Paenitentia*.

John Paul II, Pope. 1987. *Sollicitudo Rei Socialis*.

Lewis, C.S. 1961. *Screwtape letters*, New York: The Macmillan Company, 86-90.

Liguori, Alphonsus. 1952. *Uniformity with God's Will*. Prefaced and translated by Thomas W. Tobin

Teresa of Ávila. 1957. *The Life of Saint Teresa of Ávila by Herself*. Translated with an introduction by J.M. Cohen St. Ives, England: Penguin Books.

FORMATION OF A CATHOLIC PHYSICIAN

Integrating Faith and Life as a Catholic Physician

I had an interesting experience in talking to a young Catholic doctor who is undergoing residency training at the moment. His struggle is that he is working so hard and feels tired. He also can make no connection between his faith and his life as a busy intern. When I asked him, he was unable to explain any aspects of his work that would connect to his faith and worship - as if the Holy mass on Sunday was one thing and the work on Monday was totally unconnected.

I have observed this in various dialogues with various Catholic doctors and doctors-to-be (medical students) - many of them find it hard to integrate their faith and their work. I am reminded of the words of *Gaudium et Spes* regarding those

> who think that religion consists in acts of worship alone and in the discharge of certain moral obligations, and who imagine they can plunge themselves into earthly affairs in such a way as to imply that these are altogether divorced from the religious life. This split between the faith which many profess and their daily lives deserves to be counted among the more serious errors of our age. (Vatican Council II 1965, n. 43)

Rather than denounce their "serious error" I see it more of a motivation to be dedicated to their evangelization. To help the at-times overworked doctor to really value his or her own efforts, to grasp that our Lord himself values their long hours, hard work, and sacrifice, and that their self-giving is a real path to holiness and Christification.

Jesus as the Good Doctor

It is a pity and slightly ironic that a Catholic doctor has difficulty to identify or live an effective spirituality in their work place considering that in the tradition of the Church, Jesus is recognized as the "Divine Physician" and "Good Doctor" by the Church Fathers. St. Augustine cries "O my inner Physician" (Confessions, Bk 10, Ch. 3) and "Woe is me! Behold, I do not hide my wounds. Thou art the Physician, I am the sick man" (Confessions, Bk 10, Ch. 28). Jesus exercised the ministry of healing, and the gospels are littered with examples of him curing the sick. We need only remember the cure of the servant of the centurion among many others

> The centurion said in reply, "Lord, I am not worthy to have you enter under my roof; only say the word and my servant will be healed" ... And Jesus said to the centurion, "You may go; as you have believed, let it be done for you." And at that very hour his servant was healed. (Matt 8:8.13)

Jesus was a healer and even said "Those who are well do not need a physician, but the sick do" (Matt 9:12).

But the medicine of Jesus was not paracetamol but the mercy of God. So, Jesus is the Good Doctor - surely it should not be too difficult for a Catholic doctor to develop an authentic spirituality in and from his or her work as a physician?

Jesus as the Patient

A Catholic doctor is further assisted in living his/her faith in the hospital when he/she comes to the awareness that not only is Christ the Good Doctor, but he is also present in the patient. How can we understand this? The words of Jesus help us in the twenty-fifth chapter of Matthew's Gospel when the Son of Man said he was "ill and you cared for me" (Matt 25:36). The unsuspecting medics could not remember this moment so they ask "when did we see you ill?" A few verses later (in Matt 25:40) we have the clear answer "And the king will say to them in reply, 'Amen, I say to you, whatever you did for one of these least brothers of mine, you did for me.'"[1]

Knowing this, I always encourage doctors in their work telling them that they have the great privilege in their work of treating the sick, and when they touch the sick person, they are touching Christ himself. In a more mystical way, they can also recall the words in the institution of the Eucharist "This is my Body." Those words are true not only in the Mass on Sunday but also in the operating theatre or clinic on Monday.

I think as doctors we can touch the body of the patient in a different way, not just feeling for abdominal tenderness, but conscious that we are touching the body of Christ. I remember the email of a medical student from Venezuela. She is a lay member of our community and she shared how she had been involved in the treatment of a bank robber with many gunshot wounds, in Caracas. At first, she just saw the wounds and the blood loss, but she became aware in one moment that these wounds also belong to the wounded Christ of today.

Contemplatives in Action!

How do we find meaning in what we are doing as Catholic doctors? It is by finding Christ in what we are doing. Sometimes this is hard as we forget to pray! Busy doctors also need to be contemplatives in action. They are not called to spend their whole day in the convent or monastery, although at times they might enjoy the break, but they are called to be contemplatives in action. In his recent apostolic exhortation, Pope Francis said

> The problem is not always an excess of activity, but rather activity undertaken badly, without adequate motivation, without a spirituality which would permeate it and make it pleasurable. As a result, work becomes more tiring than necessary, even leading at times to illness. Far from a content and happy tiredness, this is a tense, burdensome, dissatisfying and, in the end, unbearable fatigue. (Francis 2013, n. 82)

Later he states the remedy

> What is needed is the ability to cultivate an interior space which can give a Christian meaning to commitment and activity. Without prolonged moments of adoration, of prayerful encounter with the word, of sincere conversation with the Lord, our work easily becomes meaningless; we lose energy as a result of weariness and difficulties, and our fervor dies out. The Church urgently needs the deep breath of prayer. (Francis 2013, n. 262)

We often ask our patients to take a deep breath but we need to be the first ones to take a deep breath of prayer before our work, otherwise if we are not inspired by what we are doing our enthusiasm will soon expire! We can be doing many things but it can even become tasteless.

Without Prayer our Work becomes Tasteless

I remember once being assigned to cook dinner for my fellow missionaries. I decided to make a tasty soup. I found some chicken, some leftover vegetables and flung all the ingredients into a big pot and decided to call it "Scottish soup." It was lacking salt and so, after adding some, still it did not taste right, so I poured in the rest of the bag. Serving the soup, the others commented that it was great but it lacked salt. I protested that I had put in half a bag. This caused some confusion as one brother in charge of the kitchen supplies said that actually we had no salt in the house. I checked the bag and it was not salt but Ajinomoto, a type of monosodium glutamate food flavor enhancer. When there is no salt all is tasteless! "You are the salt of the earth, but if salt loses its saltiness..." (see Matt 5:13). I think the salt in our Christian lives is prayer, downtime, or moments of reflection.

Was it 154 Stitches?

I am sharing these things to you in hindsight really. When I was working full time as a doctor I never really prayed. I was not a holy as I am now! I studied medicine at Cambridge University in England. At the end of my first year, my supervisor wrote in his report "This boy knows absolutely no anatomy whatsoever. However, his ambition to be a surgeon should be taken seriously." Seven years later I was a doctor, teaching anatomy at Edinburgh University preparing for my fellowship in surgery which I passed. The Lord called me when I was doing my specialization in plastic surgery.

How is it possible, the passage from plastics to priesthood? Simple! At first, I understood my call as a surgeon "Reconstruct my people," and so I did that. But I also began to reflect on my experiences, at least some of them. Not quite a contemplative in action but on the way. One Saturday night we treated a drunk man who had been fighting with his neighbor. He had been struck on the head by a beer bottle and required surgery to his multiple scalp lacerations. At 3 am, I was assisting and also tasked with counting the sutures for our subsequent police report. A sudden drowsiness came over me, and I had to ask my boss "Was it 153 or 154 stitches?" A few days later the beautiful wife of the patient entered the ward. She seemed very attractive until she found out the story. She turned to me in her fury. "Just wait until next Saturday! That neighbor of ours is going to need more than 300 stitches!" "Oh dear," I thought "more work for us!"

Reconstruct my People

I was struck by something. I had fixed the face (and scalp) of our drunken brawler but who was going to fix that face of hatred of the wife? That hatred and ugliness was the cause of the violence. How to fix that? The dim light of a calling dawned on me - to reconstruct the face of Christ in this person. To dedicate to reconstruction, to pass from a fisherman to a fisher of men, to pass from a reconstructive surgeon to reconstruct the people of God! It was not a change but rather a deepening of the calling I had always felt. To reconstruct the face of Christ in the world in the lives of many. I say it is not really a change although of course a slight change in the salary from a plastic surgeon in training to a priest with a vow of poverty. That is why I am always happy to take donations!

The mission of the Church then is the great project of the Holy Spirit to reconstruct and renew the face of the earth. That is why every Pentecost when we pray "Come Holy Spirit and renew the face of the earth" I always add quietly under my breath "and renew this face as well."

Intellectual Formation

Coupled with spiritual formation is the intellectual formation of the Catholic physician. Most doctors today are very well prepared and for this we had to sit many exams, reviews, board exams, etc. But how about our Catholic formation? Sometimes we can be medically updated, but in the medical world of today are we updated with all its ethical challenges?

Key "Catholic" Areas

I think there are some key issues which every Catholic physician should be well versed in, updated, and able to explain:

1. To be aware of the medical / psychological / sociological consequences of abortion;

2. To be able to explain why in vitro fertilization is wrong;

3. To know the medical and moral pitfalls of contraception;

4. To be able to promote natural family planning;

5. To be updated on HIV and AIDS rates worldwide and be familiar with how to assist the most at-risk populations (MARPS);

6. To advise against physician-assisted suicide and euthanasia;

7. To beware of receiving luxurious gifts from pharmaceutical companies;

8. To have more concern for the health care of the poor;

9. To recognize the victims of human trafficking and prostitution when we see them in the emergency room or in our practices.

Doctors have a Powerful Voice

Many in society still respect the opinion of the physician. One example from overseas is the role of doctors in campaigning to reduce alcohol consumption in Scotland, for example by lobbying to reduce sponsorship of sporting events by alcoholic brands.

In Scotland, on one day (Grant 2011,2):

- Alcohol will cost Scotland £97.5 million in terms of health, violence, and crime;
- Alcohol will kill five people;
- 98 people will be admitted to hospital with an alcohol-related condition;
- 23 people will commit a drunk driving offence;
- 450 victims of violent crime will perceive their assailant to be under the influence of alcohol.

What Can be Done? Something!

The doctors in Scotland worked on areas such as pricing of alcohol, information and education, labeling of alcohol products, and early intervention and treatment of alcohol misuse.

We Cannot Just Keep Quiet

I was shocked to read the news regarding the Australian euthanasia advocate Dr. Philip Nitschke. He was suspended from the medical register for helping a forty-five-year-old man to die. What surprised me was the resilience of Dr. Nitschke to continue his deathly ministry!

Formation of a Catholic Physician

Even when told he would be suspended, he said "It will make no difference to what I do." While he is shouting to the world and hastening the death of many, we as physicians for life cannot remain silent! As the pastor and theologian Dietrich Bonhoeffer also noted

> Silence in the face of evil is itself evil: God will not hold us guiltless. Not to speak is to speak. Not to act is to act. Each one of us should do our part.

As St. Paul exhorts Timothy and each one of us,

> Proclaim the word; be persistent whether it is convenient or inconvenient; convince, reprimand, encourage through all patience and teaching. For the time will come when people will not tolerate sound doctrine but, following their own desires and insatiable curiosity, will accumulate teachers and will stop listening to the truth and will be diverted to myths. But you, be self-possessed in all circumstances; put up with hardship; perform the work of an evangelist; fulfill your ministry. (2 Tim 4:2-5)

I continue to pray for the good formation, both spiritual and intellectual, not just of physicians but Catholic physicians.

Note

1. In these words' recent bioethics documents of the Magisterium also see the human embryo included, being truly the smallest and least amongst men. See CDF (2008, n. 37), also John Paul II (1995, n. 104) and CDF (1987, Conclusion).

References

Congregation for the Doctrine of the Faith (CDF). 1987. *Donum vitae.*

Congregation for the Doctrine of the Faith (CDF). 2008. *Dignitas personae.*

Francis, Pope. 2013. *Evangelii Gaudium.*

Grant, Gail. 2011. BMA Scotland Briefing: "One Day" alcohol campaign. Edinburgh, Scotland: BMA Scotland.

John Paul II, Pope. 1995. *Evangelium vitae.*

Vatican Council II. 1965. *Gaudium et Spes.*

GET UP, YOUNG MAN, AND LIVE!

Before I became a priest, I worked in a hospital. I was a medical doctor for seven years. I studied medicine at Cambridge University and received my medical degree in 1992. I wanted to be a surgeon, because I thought that it was the greatest thing! I did not give much attention to spiritual things - only sometimes to drinking spirits on a night out with other doctors.

I did my internship in general surgery, working in different departments to get experience: emergency room, laparoscopic surgery, breast surgery, intensive care unit, and vascular surgery. I also did orthopedic surgery - elective and trauma. I passed my board exam in general surgery. After that I did some plastic surgery and decided to specialize in it. That is why I am so handsome today! Actually, this beauty is 100 percent natural.

At that time, I had a good career, money, friends, a house, and a car. I was celebrating my birthday with some friends, and there was some music in the background. I was singing along to a song of U2 - "I still haven't found what I'm looking for, I still haven't found what I'm looking for." One of my friends asked me, "Is it true?"

"What?"

"You still haven't found what you're looking for."

I thought, "Don't blame me, I didn't write the song. You need to discuss it with Bono."

But after a while I thought, it is true. Even with all these things of the world, I am not fulfilled - I am not happy. It can happen to any health care worker. One is working very hard, but it feels that something is lacking. Have you ever felt like that? Jesus once said, "What is the point of winning the whole world but losing your life?" I felt like that.

A Plan for Life

Around that time, I met some Sisters of the Verbum Dei Fraternity, Catholic missionaries who were dedicated to sharing the Word of God.

I went to a meditation, and they shared a passage from the prophet Jeremiah: "I alone know the plans I have for you, plans to give you happiness and not disaster, plans to give you the future you want" (Jeremiah 29:11). I was struck - no one had ever told me that there was a plan for my life. I felt there was one, but no one could tell me what it was, not my parents, my friends, or my boss . . . only God, but I had never listened to Him! Verse 13 of Jeremiah 29 says, "Seek me and you will find me, if you seek me with all your heart." That was the problem! I had not been looking for God - but He found me.

I started to nourish myself every day with the living bread of the Word of God - and of course, when you begin to nourish yourself spiritually, you can help to nourish others. You also see events differently, and you see your patients differently.

Get up, Young Man, and Live!

I remember one day in the hospital in Sydney, I was called down to the emergency room to see a young man of twenty-six who had cut his wrists and wanted to end his life. This was not the first time I had come across a case like this - in fact, covering hand injuries, I had seen quite a few. But because I was praying, I saw things differently. I asked the Lord why these young people are not happy. They don't want to live. They don't have life. I remember in the Gospel when Jesus shouted at a young man who was lifeless, "Young man, get up!" I felt the same toward this boy.

He needed an eight-hour operation to reconstruct his wrists, as he had cut everything. After his operation, I told him that the reconstruction went well and that we had fixed his hand. He started to cry. I wondered why. He said, "You fixed my hand, but who will fix my life?" From then on, I desired to dedicate my life in the mission to announcing the Gospel to these many sad people, shouting out, "Young man, I tell you, get up!" Get up and live, get up and make the most of this short life.

In leaving my career I decided that others can take care of the physical life, but I am going to dedicate my life to the eternal life, the life with a capital L.

It is interesting to me, as a missionary priest, to see how the good Lord makes use of all I received. One day after a Mass in Singapore, a beautiful woman approached me to seek some beauty tips. "Doctor, I mean Father, I heard in your homily that you were a plastic surgeon. Can you give me some beauty tips?"

I responded, "Well, I shouldn't really give away any tricks of the trade, but it all depends on the daily face cream you use."

She told me that every day she was using face cream with vitamins C and D. I told her that this was a waste of time. What is best is vitamin P.

"What is that? I have never heard of it. What is this Vitamin P that keeps you young and vivacious?"

"Vitamin Prayer!" I told her. That is what we need to stay young and beautiful.

Health Care and the "Three Hs"

We have all heard the expression "You are what you eat." St. Paul said, "If you sow in the field of the Spirit, you will reap in the field of the Spirit." What you sow is what you will reap - a healthy spiritual life leads to a healthy moral life. Three ethical areas of concern to all health care workers are honesty, humility, and a heart for humanity.

Honesty is the professional integrity to do the best one can in one's job, to be honest in front of God, yourself, your colleagues, and your patients. Am I doing my job to the best of my capacity, talents, and ability? Is my heart in it? One doctor told me she was feeling bad because she was charting details about patients but not actually visiting them. We need to take care, because shortcuts can be dangerous.

Another value that is important is humility. There is a joke: What is the difference between a surgeon and God? God does not think he is a surgeon. Jesus said,

Get up, Young Man, and Live!

"The greater you are, the more you must humble yourselves." And maybe we should say that the greater you think you are, the more you must humble yourself!

Sometimes we go gaga over titles. As a seminarian, I went to visit the Rotary Club, seeking sponsors for our theology studies.

"Father James, welcome!"

"It is not Father but brother."

"Father James, meet my friends."

"It is Brother."

"Father James - what? You are just a brother?"

"Yes, I told you."

"Oh, I thought you were a father." (I thought she was going to cry.) "I didn't know you were only a brother."

"Yes, I am only a brother."

Then a friend of hers arrived.

"Have you already met Doctor James?"

"Doctor James? I thought he was only Brother James."

"No, he's not just Brother James, he is Doctor James."

"Doctor James, I didn't know he was Doctor James."

"Not just a doctor, but a plastic surgeon!"

JESUS THE DIVINE PHYSICIAN

"A plastic surgeon. Wow! I didn't know he was a plastic surgeon. Can you fix my nose?"

"No need, you are beautiful already."

There is a theological doctrine called *imago Dei* - that each person is made in the image and likeness of God. "God made man in his image and likeness" (Genesis 1:26). It is vital to recognize the dignity of each person. Do I recognize this *imago Dei* or only the title?

Another important virtue for health care workers is to have a heart - a heart for humanity. A startling reality in health care in many countries is that many people will never see a doctor during their entire lives. While some can receive the latest care, others receive none at all. This is a serious ethical concern for each one of us.

Concern for the Poor

I was very shocked going to visit homes in the depressed areas of the Philippines. It is incredible how many children have skin rashes. They were asking my opinion, but I am not a dermatologist! I have difficulty identifying rashes in Caucasian skin - but here in the Philippines when the missionaries tell me of a skin rash, I have to ask them to point it out. Where are all the dermatologists? Perhaps investing in making skins whiter! In the UK, everybody wants a tan and would die for brown skin, but here in Manila, white is sexy!

Why do so few doctors and nurses serve the poor? There are medical missions, but sometimes these are just to appease the conscience, like a tranquilizer or anesthetic. None of us are exempt from the responsibility to be concerned for the care of our brothers and sisters. Jesus Himself said, "When I was ill you cared for me." It is Christ Himself in the person who is sick and poor.

In one of the tenements, we saw a two-year-old girl who had died of pneumonia. We were with some British medical students. It was very hard to be in front of a coffin with a dead little girl inside. When we were leaving the tenement, the medical students asked the pharmacy how much the antibiotics would have cost. They were shocked - ninety pesos (about two U.S. dollars). Jesus died for thirty pieces of silver, but that little girl died for much less. Two weeks later I was invited out for a coffee. I enjoyed my cappuccino until I saw the price: ninety pesos.

What treatment needs to be prescribed? What is the sure remedy? To fix our eyes constantly on Jesus. He is the model for us as health care workers. We know that Jesus was very sensitive to the sick and suffering and that he did many miracles. In some ways, the work of each health care worker is a continuation of His healing ministry. Jesus wants to continue reaching out to the sick today, touching them, healing them, and curing them through your words, your hands, and your life.

May we take seriously the call of Jesus to love Him in the sick. It will be our judgment and our salvation too. In fact, your workplace is where you are also called to be holy. May you enjoy your work even though it is hard. Remember you are called to become a saint! Don't forget the vitamin P to keep you looking young and beautiful! And cultivate the virtues of honesty, humility, and a big heart for the whole of humanity, especially the poor and those who suffer the most. Amen.

LAZARUS, COME OUT!

This is a reflection based on the final sickness of a Filipino boy called David (name changed to preserve anonymity). To understand the events, it will help to read them in the light of chapter 11 of the Gospel of John, when Jesus raised the dead man, Lazarus. Today there are many questions in front of suffering. Why suffering? Why do people die? If God has power, why does he not do what he did for Lazarus to more people? What is Jesus trying to teach us? Ultimately, it is a message about life and its meaning.

Gospel of John - the Raising of Lazarus

[1]Now a man was ill, Lazarus from Bethany, the village of Mary and her sister Martha. [2]So the sisters sent word to him, saying, "Master, the one you love is ill." [3]When Jesus heard this he said, "This illness is not to end in death, but is for the glory of God, that the Son of God may be glorified through it…". [5]Jesus loved Martha and her sister and Lazarus…

[11]Jesus said "Our friend Lazarus is asleep, but I am going to awaken him." [12]So the disciples said to him, "Master, if he is asleep, he will be saved." [13]But Jesus was talking about his death, while they thought that he meant ordinary sleep. [14]So then Jesus said to them clearly, "Lazarus has died. [15]And I am glad for you that I was not there, that you may believe. Let us go to him."

[20]When Martha heard that Jesus was coming, she went to meet him, but Mary sat at home. [21]Martha said to

Jesus, "Lord, if you had been here, my brother would not have died. ²²But even now I know that whatever you ask of God, God will give you." ²³Jesus said to her, "Your brother will rise." ²⁴Martha said to him, "I know he will rise, in the resurrection on the last day." ²⁵Jesus told her, "I am the resurrection and the life; whoever believes in me, even if he dies, will live, ²⁶and everyone who lives and believes in me will never die. Do you believe this?"...

³²When Mary came to where Jesus was and saw him, she fell at his feet and said to him, "Lord, if you had been here, my brother would not have died." ³³When Jesus saw her weeping and the Jews who had come with her weeping, he became perturbed and deeply troubled, and said, "Where have you laid him?" They said to him, "Sir, come and see."... ³⁵And Jesus wept.

³⁸So Jesus, perturbed again, came to the tomb. It was a cave, and a stone lay across it. ³⁹Jesus said, "Take away the stone." Martha, the dead man's sister, said to him, "Lord, by now there will be a stench; he has been dead for four days." ⁴⁰Jesus said to her, "Did I not tell you that if you believe you will see the glory of God?" ⁴¹So they took away the stone. And Jesus raised his eyes and said, "Father, I thank you for hearing me. ⁴²I know that you always hear me, but because of the crowd here I have said this, that they may believe that you sent me." ⁴³And when he had said this, he cried out in a loud voice, "Lazarus, come out!" ⁴⁴The dead man came out, tied hand and foot with burial bands, and his face was wrapped in a cloth.

Lazarus, Come Out!

So Jesus said to them, "Untie him and let him go." (excerpts from John 11:1-44)

Lazarus, come out!

There was knock at the door. It was one of the local boys with blood dripping from his nose. He had come to us as he had no one else to turn to. His name was David, from a very poor family. He was twenty-four years old. We went to the hospital where he was diagnosed with anemia. He needed five bags of blood for a transfusion. I discovered then that here in the Philippines there are no free blood banks, you have to pay or provide the blood yourself. Seeing as each bag was two weeks wages and we did not have any money, we gathered five missionaries to donate blood. I was struck by the poster on the wall of the hospital "Give blood. Give life!" There was a call to give life in this situation. I looked at the different faces of my missionary brothers and wondered how David would react to blood from five different countries. His blood would be "the united colors of Benetton." The good news was that he responded well to the transfusion and afterwards his color returned. The very bad news was that he was diagnosed with aplastic anemia.

That night at supper, I noticed how much the missionaries who had given blood were eating and drinking. The next day I found myself exhausted and dehydrated. I discovered the hard way that after giving blood you need to drink a bit more to replace the lost fluid, especially in the heat. "Thanks for telling me," I said to my brothers. "You should know that; you are the doctor!" they replied.

We tried hard over the next year to help him, but it was not easy as there is no real cure. The only cure would be a bone marrow transplant but at $75,000 it was virtually impossible. Attempts to raise funds through an appeal on radio or through the newspapers proved futile. Every three months he had a bleeding crisis, needing five bags or more of blood. His blood count was very low which meant his body was a ticking time bomb - the slightest injury could mean he might bleed to death. It was a precious year of life for him and for his family. One day he bumped his head on a cupboard, suffered a cerebral hemorrhage, and went into a coma. At the government hospital, it was like a scene from a war zone. So many patients seriously injured. The hard-working staff were trying to resuscitate an old man who had fallen out of a coconut tree. Collecting coconuts had been his livelihood for over fifty years. I looked at David and asked God to give us strength to help him, as I had been doing since the day we met him. "Help us please Lord. Why does it have to be like this? Why all this suffering? Why don't you manifest your power?" I remembered Jesus when his friend Lazarus was sick

> "This illness is not to end in death, but is for the glory of God... If you believe you will see the glory of God." Jesus raised his eyes and said "Father, I thank you for hearing me. I know that you always hear me; but because of the crowd here I have said this, that they may believe that

Lazarus, Come Out!

you sent me." And when he had said this, he cried out in a loud voice, "Lazarus, come out!" The dead man came out, tied hand and foot with burial bands, and his face was wrapped in a cloth. (John 11:3, 40-44)

I asked Jesus "If you could do that then, why don't you do the same now?" At that moment, David regained consciousness and opened his eyes. I prayed "Oh Jesus, it's really true, you are the resurrection and the life."

But with a platelet count of less than ten, this boy was on borrowed time. The ninety minutes were up, and now it was extra-time. But what for? Why was he allowed to live a bit longer? We took the boy home, and it happened that on the way back we encountered a monsoon. The terrible rain could not dampen our spirits. We were so joyous to bring him home to his mother, probably for the last time. The final walk to his house was about one and half miles over very hilly terrain. We had brought five pairs of bright yellow waterproofs. As the five of us (David, his two sisters, Br. Vic another missionary, and I) traipsed our way home, I could not help thinking that we must have looked like five martians from outer space with our bright yellow waterproofs on in the pouring rain. As I looked at David, trying to keep going I was amazed to think that in most other countries he would have had an ambulance to take him home, but here he was having just received six bags of blood coming back in a monsoon.

JESUS THE DIVINE PHYSICIAN

As we made our way up the hill in one column, David was in front and I was pushing him up the hill and behind me, pushing me and David up the hill was Br. Vic, my Filipino brother. With torrents of water flowing down the hill, we started to lose our grip and slide down the hill. In that moment, I looked over my shoulder to see Br. Vic straining, all fifty kilos of him - "Push harder," I shouted. He mustered strength from somewhere, and with an almighty shove we were on our way again, before arriving safely at the little house of David.

The borrowed time lasted seven days. He spent the last week with his family, and after that he was admitted again to the hospital with a major brain hemorrhage. Br. Vic and I went back to the hospital for the last time. On entering his room we were greeted with a gruesome scene. David was fitting, having a major seizure. It was not pleasant to see especially for his two helpless sisters. They were so distressed, and I remembered Martha and Mary, the sisters of Lazarus, and how they wept at the death of their brother, and Jesus showed us his humanity and wept too. Phenytoin, the antidote had been prescribed by the doctor, but there was no money to buy it. "Why did you prescribe a medicine when you know that they can't afford it?" I asked the doctor. Perhaps I was a bit angry. He was doing his best, but somehow it did not seem enough. The medicine cost $1. "Can you lend me the money?" I asked him. "I promise I will pay you back." He was a bit shocked.

Lazarus, Come Out!

After the injection, David settled down and entered into the twilight zone of life - the final passage from here to eternity. His family told me that this last week had been beautiful. One brother had come from a long way away to be united with the family. The family were as one. I saw the work and the wisdom of God. Perhaps David was not only alive for himself, but for others too, and this was his final mission - to unite his family and finish the work of the One who sent him. The person who seems weakest and helpless is often the one who is helping others the most. He was fighting for breath now, gasping. I looked at his face. He was someone abandoned and rejected by the society at large, like many of the poor in our world today. His body was so thin and weak now, full of injection marks. I remembered the events of that last year. What a fight to save this boy. Somehow all seemed to be in vain. Where was the victory? Death had won at last?

I realized that in all my years before in the hospital I have never felt like this. I had never really fought for someone's life. But for this boy, I had given my blood. When I looked at the drops of blood coming from his injection sites, I realized that it was partly mine. This life had cost me. It was a miracle that we had endured. How many times Jesus was telling me, "*Love to the very end*" just like he did. Not to give up. So many times I wanted to give up and die, but Jesus brought me to life again. I had wanted to give up because it seemed useless, but a big hand had been pushing me on. Not just Br. Vic's hand, but a slightly bigger one.

JESUS THE DIVINE PHYSICIAN

Only in prayer can we find the strength to endure. It is where Jesus reaches out his hand and tells us to get up. Good intentions are just not enough. When you want to give up, Jesus will give you the strength to go on. I had seen people die, but I was never really so affected. But this time, I really wanted this boy to live. His breathing became heavier, coming in deep gasps. I looked at his face. I saw the face of Jesus and listened to those words "*I thirst*" (John 19:28). I heard the deep cry of Jesus "*Lazarus, come out!*" Come out and live. This life is so short and precious. Do not be afraid to live it. I want you to live. The one who was being called to live this moment was me. This extra time was not only for David but for me, to learn how to live.

Time has passed since his death. I continue to pray for him and his family. He made me realize the beauty and dignity of each life - that life is worth fighting for. We are living in a society that does not seem to value life. That judges it on performance. Even, many are calling for euthanasia for those who suffer. Why are people allowed to suffer? Perhaps it is for you and me, to give us life and to teach us how to love, to the very end. When a society does not react any more to the suffering of others, perhaps it is because it is dying. A society that supports euthanasia is already dead. Wake us up from our tombs, Jesus. You saw the value of each life and you were prepared to give your life for each one. Teach us how to live, teach us how to love. I realize that if you want to make a difference in the world of today, you need to prepare for a challenge. In front of big challenges, you need a big love - the

Lazarus, Come Out!

love of Christ. And there is no greater love than this, to give your life for your friends.

Thank you, Jesus, for the miracle of life - help us to use our borrowed time wisely, teach us how to be fully alive. Jesus said "I am the resurrection and the life, whoever believes in me will never die" (John 11:25), and St. Paul tells us also

> If the Spirit of the one who raised Jesus from the dead dwells in you, the one who raised Christ from the dead will give life to your mortal bodies also, through his Spirit that dwells in you. (Romans 8:11)

"And when he had said this, he cried out in a loud voice, 'Lazarus, come out!'" Come out, James, come out my friend. I am shouting, loudly. Can you hear me? Yes, Jesus, I can hear you. Come out into the light. Come out of your tomb. I created you to live. Come out of your tomb of complacency and comfort. Don't be afraid to love, to give your blood, to give your life. Complicate your life a little bit. *"The dead man came out, tied hand and foot with burial bands, and his face was wrapped in a cloth."* Take the bandage of fear from your eyes, that stops you seeing the real needs of others. Do not be afraid to love them, to make mistakes, I will catch you if you fall. Do not be afraid to die. I am the giver of Life! Time is short. The evening draws near. I want you to live.

So Jesus said to them, 'Untie him and let him go.'" I have saved you and I have brought you back to life many times. Go and live this short life to the full. Do not be afraid to give your life. So many people are afraid to love, do not be afraid to love, to give your life. I am with you always; I will help you. I want nothing less for your life - "*There is no greater love than this to give your life for your friends*" (John 15:13). Come out, Lazarus, and through your life, I will call many people back to life. The Lazarus was not David, you see, it was me.

SUFFERING, DEATH AND ETERNAL LIFE

I was asked to give a series of four talks to the doctors and staff of the Oncology Department at St. Luke's Medical Center, Quezon City, Manila. It was really a privilege and a joy to meet them and share with them. The theme of the talks was "Suffering, death, and eternal life." In this summary article, I would like to share some of the insights I gained. The first part focusses on suffering and the second part on death and eternal life.

Part 1 - Suffering

Doctors, their patients, and indeed every human person have, at some time or other, to confront the meaning of suffering. As Pope Saint John Paul II noted, suffering is "almost inseparable from man's earthly existence" (John Paul II 1984, n. 3). Why do we suffer? Is there a deeper meaning? What light does Christian faith shed on the mystery of suffering?

From a faith point of view, we can say that in the initial state, in the Garden of Eden, there was no suffering. Suffering came in with sin and the fall. The *Catechism* explains "as a result of original sin, human nature is weakened in its powers, subject to ignorance, suffering, and the domination of death, and inclined to sin (this inclination is called 'concupiscence')" (Catechism 1997, n. 418).

JESUS THE DIVINE PHYSICIAN

In the Light of Christ

Pope Saint John Paul II wrote an apostolic letter called *Salvifici Doloris* on the Christian meaning of human suffering. In number fifteen it states:

> And even though the victory over sin and death achieved by Christ in his Cross and Resurrection does not abolish temporal suffering from human life, nor free from suffering the whole historical dimension of human existence, it nevertheless throws a new light upon this dimension and upon every suffering: the light of salvation. (John Paul II 1984, n. 15)

The *Catechism for Filipino Catholics* poses a much-asked question "If God is 'Father' and 'Almighty,' why does He allow so much evil and suffering?" (Catholic Bishops' Conference of the Philippines 1997, n. 309). The answers, given by the same *Catechism*, are both comforting and enlightening:

> First, much evil in the world, especially *physical* evil, results from the kind of *limited* universe in which we live.

> Second, moral evil and much of human suffering come from man's abuse of his freedom in sin.

> Third, much courage, generosity, forgiveness, hope, and sacrifice arise from the world's sufferings and evils.

Finally, Christ's Paschal Mystery shows how God draws out of the depths of evil the victory of the Risen Christ and his transforming love.

Suffering and Sickness

> Illness and suffering have always been among the gravest problems confronted in human life. In illness, man experiences his powerlessness, his limitations, and his finitude. Every illness can make us glimpse death.
>
> Illness can lead to anguish, self-absorption, sometimes even despair and revolt against God. It can also make a person more mature, helping him discern in his life what is not essential so that he can turn toward that which is. Very often illness provokes a search for God and a return to him. (Catechism 1997, nn. 1500-1501)

Suffering as Sharing in His Redemption

Pope Saint John Paul II explained how suffering can be understood as a sharing in the redemption of Christ.

> The Redeemer suffered in place of man and for man. Every man has his own share in the Redemption. Each one is also called to share in that suffering through which the Redemption was accomplished. He is called to share in that suffering through which all human suffering has also been redeemed. In bringing about the Redemption through suffering, Christ has also raised human suffering to the level of the Redemption. Thus each man, in his suffering,

can also become a sharer in the redemptive suffering of Christ. (John Paul II 1984, n. 19)

St. Paul and the Meaning of Suffering

The letters and understanding of Paul reveal some interesting details of the meaning of Christian suffering. Perhaps three key words can summarize a triple perspective he gives to the meaning of suffering - struggle, strength, and hope:

• *Struggle.* In his second letter to the Corinthians, Paul writes: "We are afflicted in every way, but not crushed; perplexed, but not driven to despair; persecuted, but not forsaken; struck down, but not destroyed; always carrying in the body the death of Jesus, so that the life of Jesus may also be manifested in our bodies" (2 Cor 4:8-10).

• *Strength.* "That I may know him [Christ] and the power of his Resurrection, and may share his sufferings, becoming like him in his death, that if possible, I may attain the resurrection from the dead" (Phil 3:10-11). Paul draws his strength in suffering from the Risen Christ.

• *Hope.* "More than that, we rejoice in our sufferings, knowing that suffering produces endurance, and endurance produces character, and character produces hope, and hope does not disappoint us, because God's love has been poured into our hearts through the Holy Spirit which has been given to us" (Rom 5:3-5). In various moments Paul alludes to the virtue of hope as being a necessary requisite to endure the challenges.

To Personalize Our Suffering

What can make suffering more acute is when it is perceived that there is no meaning to it. Viktor Frankl, an Austrian neurologist and psychiatrist, spent three years in various concentration camps during World War II. In *Man's Search for Meaning*, a book based on his experience of imprisonment at Auschwitz and various subsidiary camps of Dachau, he writes,

> when a man finds that it is his destiny to suffer, he will to have accept his suffering as his task; his single and unique task. He will have to acknowledge the fact that even in his suffering he is unique and alone in the universe. No one can relieve him of his suffering or suffer in his place. His unique opportunity lies in the way in which he bears his burden. (Frankl 2006, 77-78)

The apostle Peter had to personalize his call to pick up the cross and follow Christ. When Jesus first passes by the Sea of Galilee, he invites Peter, and his brother Andrew, "Come, follow me" (see Matt 4:18-19). Later, after the death and resurrection of Christ, the risen Lord again invites Peter to "Follow me" (John 21:19). It is very interesting what happens next. Peter turns and sees the disciple Jesus loved and asks Jesus "What about him?" Jesus tells Peter, "Never you mind about him. You follow me" (see John 21:20-22). Peter is easily distracted. Perhaps it can be a sign of the challenge to personalize our own calling. What is the Lord asking me, not others? Like Peter, we can become distracted and too busy looking at others instead of answering his call to us. His brother, Andrew, is attested by tradition to have been crucified diagonally. The "St. Andrew's cross" can be seen on the flag of Scotland. It reminds us of the need to personalize our own cross because it comes in many shapes and sizes. What is a cross for one may not be so for another. Holy Spirit, help us to pick up our cross, to personalize it, and make it our own.

The Good Samaritan

In confronting suffering the question to ask is not merely "why?" but also "what can we do about it?" I remember once talking with a lady who was very moved with many tears about suffering children in Africa. But behind the tears and strong feelings there was no action at all. The impression I got was one of a form of selfishness. Our compassion needs to move us! The Good Samaritan was moved by compassion. He did something! Not only were his feelings moved but also his will - he was moved to action, to responding, to doing something to alleviate the suffering of another. It is good to examine if my concern, my feelings, my compassion actually move me to respond.

Salvifici Doloris beautifully highlights some aspects of our needed response in front of suffering. Selected insights are quoted in full below:

- "We are not allowed to 'pass by on the other side' indifferently; we must 'stop' beside him. The name 'Good Samaritan' fits *every individual who is sensitive to the sufferings of others*, who 'is moved' by the misfortune of another" (John Paul II 1984, n. 28).

• "Therefore one must cultivate this sensitivity of heart, which bears witness to *compassion* towards a suffering person. Nevertheless, the Good Samaritan of Christ's parable does not stop at sympathy and compassion alone" (John Paul II 1984, n. 28).

• "Following the parable of the Gospel, we could say that suffering, which is present under so many different forms in our human world, is also present in order *to unleash love in the human person*" (John Paul II 1984, n. 29).

• "How much there is of 'the Good Samaritan' in the profession of the doctor, or the nurse, or others similar! Considering its 'evangelical' content, we are inclined to think here of a vocation rather than simply a profession" (John Paul II 1984, n. 29).

• "This parable witnesses to the fact that Christ's revelation of the salvific meaning of suffering *is in no way identified with an attitude of passivity*. Completely the reverse is true. The Gospel is the negation of passivity in the face of suffering" (John Paul II 1984, n. 30).

Sacrament of Anointing of the Sick

In a sacramental way, Christ, the Good Doctor[1] and Good Samaritan, is able to approach the patient through the sacrament of the Anointing of the Sick. The special grace of this sacrament has as its effects (Catechism 1997, n. 1532):

- the uniting of the sick person to the passion of Christ, for his own good and that of the whole Church;

- the strengthening, peace, and courage to endure in a Christian manner the sufferings of illness or old age;

- the forgiveness of sins, if the sick person was not able to obtain it through the sacrament of Penance;

- the restoration of health, if it is conducive to the salvation of his soul;

- the preparation for passing over to eternal life.

Part II - Death and Eternal Life

Death

I share an anecdote, partly humorous perhaps, to begin our reflection on the meaning of death. Once while doing a stint in the emergency room, I reviewed a teenage girl who was admitted with tachycardia (a raised heart rate.) I recognized her from a previous visit two weeks earlier when she had presented to the emergency room having dropped a ten-pin bowling ball on her head. She had chosen a ball with finger holes that were too small. After a hefty swing the ball had failed to release because her fingers were stuck in the holes. Her swing continued until the ball struck her on the head.

This time, her tachycardia had been caused by taking an excess of asthma inhaler "for fun" as she put it. She was really trying to impress her accompanying friends as I attempted to make her realize how serious a tachycardia could be. "Young lady, your normal heart rate should be around eighty beats per minute. The sound you hear now is the heart rate monitor going at 185 beats per minute." Still she made light of events even joking that she should have taken more of her inhaler.

I reassured her that this might not have been a good idea. "Young lady, if that was the case the sound of the heart monitor would be different. It would be a continuous beep, but anyway you would not have heard it because you would be dead." With that she burst into tears, and I left the room feeling a little guilty. Suddenly, outside the room, I heard the flat line trace. "Oh no," I thought, as I raced back into the room. On entering she sat bolt upright in bed, wide-eyed and screamed out "Doctor, am I dead? Am I dead?" To much relief, mine and hers, I reassured that she was not dead but simply that the lead for the heart-rate monitor had fallen off from her chest.

What Is Death?

Pope Saint John Paul II, addressing the Eighteenth International Congress of the Transplantation Society, said: "This gives rise to one of the most debated issues in contemporary bioethics, as well as to serious concerns in the minds of ordinary people. I refer to the problem of *ascertaining the fact of death*. When can a person be considered dead with complete certainty?" (John Paul II 2000, n. 4). From a theological point of view, the *Catechism of the Catholic Church* states that human death is "the separation of the soul from the body" (Catechism 1997, n. 997). John Haas writes,

> The reason no scientific technique can directly identify the moment of death is quite simple: the soul is a non-corporeal, spiritual life-principle which cannot be observed or measured or weighed using the tools of empirical science. The presence or absence of the soul can be ascertained only by observing certain biological signs that indirectly attest to its presence or its absence. (Haas 2011, 285)

Pope Saint John Paul II explains well the connection between death, the separation of the soul from the body, and the accompanying medical signs:

> *the death of the person* is a single event, consisting in the total disintegration of that unitary and integrated whole that is the personal self. It results from the separation of the life-principle (or soul) from the corporal reality of the person. The death of the person, understood in this primary sense, is an event which *no scientific technique or empirical method can identify directly.* Yet human experience shows that once death occurs *certain biological signs inevitably follow*, which medicine has learnt to recognize with increasing precision. In this sense, the "criteria" for ascertaining death used by medicine today should not be understood as the technical-scientific determination of the *exact moment* of a person's death, but as a scientifically secure means of identifying *the biological signs that a*

person has indeed died. (John Paul II 2000, n. 4)

What Happens Spiritually at the Moment of Death?

One day, during my residency training in plastics and reconstruction, a patient with eighty percent burns asked me outright "What do you think happens after we die?" This young man was seriously ill with an infection and in danger of death. It had been long day for me, and I just wanted to finish my shift on the burns unit and go home. He repeated his question, this time with more intensity and followed up by asking "How would you feel if you were in my situation?" I told him I could not imagine that. He persisted in his line of questioning and I felt obliged at least to try and respond truthfully.

Perhaps for the first time ever as a doctor, I explicitly shared my faith in the hospital. I said "Well one thing that comforts me in front of death is my faith in eternal life." He inquired further what this meant. I explained that I believed that life does not end with death but instead death marks a new beginning, a life in God which will last forever. I even remembered a line Jesus said: "I am the Resurrection and the Life. Whoever believes in me will live forever." I left for home feeling peaceful seeing how intently our young friend had listened to what I shared.

The next day, coming to work early, I was surprised to notice that the patient's name was no longer on his door. His mother came out of his room, looking tired and teary eyed. "My son died last night. Thank you."

I was taken aback to find out that her son had passed away. I was also slightly confused as to why she was thanking me, after all her son had died despite our best medical efforts. She continued "My son knew the end was near, and for that he was so restless. He could not find peace. But last night I came to see him. For the first time in months, I found him at peace. He told me you had spoken to him. Thank you for what you shared." Perhaps for the first time I realized the power of our faith. Not only to look at life and death through a medical perspective but also a spiritual one.

It is beautiful that we can have recourse to our faith to help us explain things which medical science cannot explain. No medical textbook, staying strictly in the realms of medical science, can give any answer to this young man. Medicine remains silent and in ignorance in front of such questions. It simply has, and will never have - despite all the advances in technology - anything more to add. The *Catechism* however can tell us "Each man receives his eternal retribution in his immortal soul at the very moment of his death, in a particular judgment that refers his life to Christ: either entrance into the blessedness of heaven through a purification or immediately - or immediate and everlasting damnation" (Catechism 1997, n. 1022).

Death in Different Cultures

The cultural context of death is vitally important. Death can be seen through varying optics and different hues depending on the cultural perspective. I remember when I first arrived in the Philippines and was invited by a family to visit the cemetery on the evening of the feast of All Souls. Getting near the cemetery I was surprised to hear loud music and wondered where the party was. To my shock it was coming from among the tombstones! As we entered, I was invited to sit down... on a tomb. I nearly jumped when I felt a hand on my shoulder - not someone coming back from the dead but rather the family who had invited me offering a burger and fries to eat.

Even celebrating the memory of the faithful departed is fun in the Philippines. It is quite different to how we remember our dead in Scotland! As doctors we are influenced by cultural perspectives, with all their richness and, at times, some bias.

Eternal Life

Death is an event we will all, one day (and not too soon we hope!) have to personally face. At the moment of death, our body and soul are separated. Our soul does not fly around for forty days despite rumors to the contrary. Instead, the soul goes to experience the judgment of God.

If in a state of perfect friendship, then heaven awaits; if imperfect, then purgatory; and somewhere hot down below if we have definitively rejected God (hard to imagine but hell is a constant teaching of our Lord and the Church). And what happens to our body? It goes to dust but does not just stay there. We will get it back, albeit in a glorified way, at the resurrection of the dead (see 1 Cor 15:42ff).

So, this life after death is not something only to look forward to later on. This eternal life has actually already begun. We received the life of God in our baptism which means we can begin this life with God in the here and now. As I often repeat in homilies on the topic, "Don't wait until after death to start living your eternal life, as it may be too late." The life of God grows in us when we pray and when we love others.

How to Live Our Eternal Life in the Here and Now?

I wrap up with some practical ways to start living our eternal in the here and now.

Eternal life as relationship

Jesus told us what this life is: "Now this is eternal life, that they should know you, the only true God, and the one whom you sent, Jesus Christ" (John 17:3). If eternal life is a relationship, then it can be lived today. This is the gift of prayer, even on a busy day, the chance to share the daily happenings with God. We can enter into this knowledge of God, this knowing him, by sharing what we live with him each day.

Eternal life as new birth

On her deathbed St. Thérèse of Lisieux wrote, "I am not dying. I am entering life." In the Mass preface often used at funerals we hear the words "life is changed, not ended." The newness of what is eternal can be experienced each day and reminds us to not get stuck in routine and monotony. St. Paul invited the Corinthians to experience this newness when he wrote "What eye has not seen, and ear has not heard, and what has not entered the human heart, what God has prepared for those who love him" (1 Cor 2:9).

Eternal life as love

Eternal life, being a life that never ends, is also understood as love, because love is eternal. St. Paul explains,

> Love never fails. If there are prophecies, they will be brought to nothing; if tongues, they will cease; if knowledge, it will be brought to nothing. For we know partially and we prophesy partially, but when the perfect comes, the partial will pass away. When I was a child, I used to talk as a child, think as a child, reason as a child; when I became a man, I put aside childish things. At present we see indistinctly, as in a mirror, but then face to face. At present I know partially; then I shall know fully, as I am fully known. So faith, hope, love remain, these three; but the greatest of these is love (1 Cor 13:8-13).

We do not need to wait for heaven to experience a life in God and a life in love. Each loving option allows us already to become sharers in the divine nature (see 2 Pet 1:4), the divine nature of a God who is love (1 Jn 4:8).

Eternal life as good choices

Choices and options can be made so that we live our eternal life here and now. The Word of God tells us: "I set before you life and death...choose life" (see Deut

30:19). When we choose to love in the small moments of our daily lives, we are choosing to invest in eternity. We should be wise investors - do not invest only in passing things - instead invest in what will last forever.

Note

1. In the tradition of the Church, Jesus is recognized as the "Divine Physician" and "Good Doctor." See, for example, St. Augustine who cries "O my inner Physician" (Confessions, bk 10, ch. 3), and "Woe is me! Behold, I do not hide my wounds. Thou art the Physician, I am the sick man" (Confessions, bk 10, ch. 28).

References

Catechism of the Catholic Church. 1997. 2nd ed. Vatican City: Libreria Editrice Vaticana.

Catholic Bishops' Conference of the Philippines. 1997. *Catechism for Filipino Catholics.* Manila, Philippines: ECCCE Word & Life Publications.

Frankl, Viktor E. 2006. *Man's search for meaning.* Boston: Beacon Press.

Haas, John M. 2011. Catholic teaching regarding the legitimacy of neurological criteria for the determination of death. *National Catholic Bioethics Quarterly* 14.4 (Summer): 279-99.

John Paul II, Pope. 1984. *Salvifici Doloris*, On the Christian meaning of human suffering.

John Paul II, Pope. 2000. Address to the 18th International Congress of the Transplantation Society.

THE PEDIATRICIAN AS PROPHET

Summary

In the gospels, Jesus got angry with his disciples because they were hindering the children from coming to him. When the disciples tried to turn them away, Jesus said "Let the children come to me" (Matt 19:14). Our Lord spoke out on behalf of the little ones at a time when they were generally despised and ignored by society. The gospels also record specific instances of Jesus healing very sick children (see Mk 5: 22-44, 35-42). In continuing the healing ministry of Jesus today, pediatricians continue to work for the welfare of many neglected children and continue to be the voice of the voiceless. Collectively as a profession, pediatric doctors have a voice that people will listen to, and they can have an important say in some problematic issues regarding children in our world of today.

One Sunday I went with a Sister and two female lay members of our Verbum Dei community in the Philippines to give a Lenten activity at a shelter for abused girls (aged five to eighteen years old). Shortly after, I was happy to discover that an article I had written to highlight the reality of domestic abuse and the plight of abused girls had been accepted for publication in a local theological journal. A week later I found myself giving a plenary talk in a national pediatrics conference where over 6,000 pediatricians attended. A thought occurred to me: surely it is not only priests (and sisters) who are called to be speak out against the domestic abuse of minors? What about the role of pediatricians? Is it not also part of their Christian duty, independent of any legal obligations? Are there no other potential areas of advocacy for pediatric doctors? Is there not a Christian duty to speak out for the voiceless when medicine or society threatens harm? And if there is, how does a pediatrician prepare himself to take on the sometimes thankless, sometimes dangerous task of witnessing to Truth in the modern world?

The Prophetic Task of All Baptized

The prophetic task does not mean to dress in camel skin, go to the desert, and eat wild locusts and honey. Not all of us are called to be like John the Baptist, but we all have been entrusted, since our baptism, the same prophetic task and it has application in our practices as physicians as well as in our lives as Christians.

In baptism, one is baptized into the priestly, kingly, and prophetic mission of Christ. The Lord asks this of each one of us to share our faith and be salt and light in the world of today.

> You are the salt of the earth. But if salt loses its taste, with what can it be seasoned? It is no longer good for anything but to be thrown out and trampled underfoot. You are the light of the world. A city set on a mountain cannot be hidden. Nor do they light a lamp and then put

> it under a bushel basket; it is set on a lampstand, where it gives light to all in the house. Just so, your light must shine before others, that they may see your good deeds and glorify your heavenly Father. (Matt 5:13-16)

After his death, when he was no longer present physically, the risen Lord commands the disciples to continue his mission and "Go into the whole world and proclaim the gospel" (Mk 16:15). The whole world would obviously include hospitals, clinics, offices, conferences, and medical journals. The risen Lord empowers the lay people, not to just lay around but to be active in transforming the world and building up the Kingdom. This mission is laid out, not only in the Gospels but in the teaching of the Church on the role of the laity.

In *Christifideles Laici*, written by Pope St. John Paul II (1988), writing about the lay members of Christ's faithful, underlines the prophetic mission of the lay.

> Through their participation in the prophetic mission of Christ, "who proclaimed the kingdom of his Father by the testimony of his life and by the power of his world," the lay faithful are given the ability and responsibility to accept the gospel in faith and to proclaim it in word and deed, without hesitating to courageously identify and denounce evil. (n. 14).

The Pediatrician as Prophet

This teaching is rooted in the understanding of the prophetic mission of the lay faithful given to us by the Second Vatican Council.

> The laity go forth as powerful proclaimers of a faith in things to be hoped for, when they courageously join to their profession of faith a life springing from faith. This evangelization, that is, this announcing of Christ by a living testimony as well as by the spoken word, takes on a specific quality and a special force in that it is carried out in the ordinary surroundings of the world.
>
> Consequently, even when preoccupied with temporal cares, the laity can and must perform a work of great value for the evangelization of the world. (Vatican Council II 1964, n. 35)

The duty and right to evangelize is even enshrined in the Canon law of the Church. The laity

> have the right, whether as individuals or in associations, to strive so that the divine message of salvation may be known and accepted by all people throughout the world. This obligation is all the more insistent in circumstances in which only through them are people able to hear the Gospel and to know Christ. (Code of Canon Law 1983, n. 225 §1)

At times, it seems that many doctors do not take this real and significant prophetic take seriously, perhaps more interested in making a profit than being one.

JESUS THE DIVINE PHYSICIAN

Those doctors are bit like the man who turned up to the Church for the first time in years. The priest said "The Lord needs you for the good fight. Come and join his army." The man said "I am already a member of his army." The priest looked surprised and asked "Then how come I have not seen you in Church for so long?" "'Cos I am in the secret service," explained the man.

To stand up for the faith in the world of today can be challenging, especially in the medical world. The temptation for Catholic doctors can be to lay low, but it is a temptation that is to be resisted. Sometimes our faith is just too secretive. We are happy to talk about many things, even many forbidden things, but talking about the faith and how it affects our lives is too often taboo. That is why Pope Paul VI (1975) gave us all a strong reminder:

> And why should only falsehood and error, debasement and pornography have the right to be put before people and often unfortunately imposed on them by the destructive propaganda of the mass media, by the tolerance of legislation, the timidity of the good and the impudence of the wicked? The respectful presentation of Christ and His kingdom is more than the evangelizer's right; it is his duty. (n. 80)

My final source of encouragement for all pediatricians to take up the prophetic gauntlet comes from Pope Francis (2013) himself in the beautiful words of his apostolic exhortation *Evangelii Gaudium*.

In virtue of their baptism, all the members of the People of God have become missionary disciples (cf. Mt 28:19). All the baptized, whatever their position in the Church or their level of instruction in the faith, are agents of evangelization, and it would be insufficient to envisage a plan of evangelization to be carried out by professionals while the rest of the faithful would simply be passive recipients. (n. 120)

Areas of Advocacy for Pediatricians

If all baptized are expected to be actively engaged in the prophetic mission of the Church, what could be the possible areas for pediatricians specifically to exercise their prophetic task as physicians and relative to medicine? I propose the following main areas of advocacy for pediatricians (conscious that the list is by no means exhaustive): domestic abuse of children, gender confusion (life issues), abortion and in vitro fertilization (IVF; beginning of life issues), and pediatric euthanasia (end of life issue).

Domestic Abuse of Children

A worldwide phenomenon, which I will highlight from my local perspective here in the Philippines, is the domestic abuse of children. A United Nations Children's Fund (UNICEF) supported study here in 2016 reported that nearly one in five Filipino girls have been sexually abused (Council for the Welfare of Children and UNICEF 2016, 4). However, the actual figures may be higher as victims may not reveal their past history. The Cameleon NGO, which takes care of girls who have been abused, notes

> In Filipino culture, family morals remain private and children are expected to keep quiet rather than report crimes that could cause scandal or emotional devastation among relatives. This culture of silence contributes to persistent sexual abuse in the country and is adopted by the victims who submit and suffer without saying a word. (Cameleon website)

The adverse health effects of sexual abuse are varied and manifest and may include (Ramiro, Madrid, and Brown 2010, 843):

- being more likely to experience both subsequent non-consensual sex and risky consensual sexual behaviors including abortion in adolescence and early adulthood
- lifetime risks of depression
- alcohol or drug dependence
- panic disorders
- post-traumatic stress disorders (PTSD)
- suicides

Ramiro, Madrid, and Brown (2010) also report that "those who were sexually abused were 12 times more likely to engage in early sex, 9 times more likely to have early pregnancy, and 5 times more likely to attempt to commit suicide" (p. 847).

The Pediatrician as Prophet

The silence surrounding abuse is one of the major driving forces in its persistence. There is a tendency to never address this topic. It remains taboo, unspoken, and is thus allowed to thrive and fester in the darkness. As John's gospel tells us "For everyone who does wicked things hates the light and does not come toward the light, so that his works might not be exposed" (Jn 3:20). Part of the work of evangelization is to bring evil deeds to the light.

There may be strong cultural tendencies that hinder our evangelizing efforts. In the gospels, we encounter the demon of silence which made the one possessed mute: "As they were going out, a demoniac who could not speak was brought to Jesus, and when the demon was driven out the mute person spoke. The crowds were amazed and said, 'Nothing like this has ever been seen in Israel'" (Matt 9:32-33, see also Lk 11:14). In an analogous way, the demon of silence makes the subject of incest taboo such that one is simply prevented from speaking about it. In fact, in the Filipino language, there is no direct word for "incest." We do not want to hear about it and remain largely deaf to the silent cry of many victims. This demon of silence still needs to be driven out today: Jesus rebuked the unclean spirit and said "Mute and deaf spirit, I command you: come out of him and never enter him again!" (Mk 9:25)

Although other countries have made progress in defeating this demon of silence, by reporting requirements and by public advocacy, it remains difficult for victims to speak out, in part because of the pain and shame of what has happened and in part, because victims are still often not believed.

The voice of pediatricians can help dispel this silence and make the victim heard. As the prophet Isaiah announced, "For Zion's sake I will not keep silent, and for Jerusalem's sake I will not be quiet, until her righteousness goes forth as brightness, and her salvation as a burning torch" (Is 62:1). Every doctor knows that prevention is better than cure and in the United States, the obligation to speak is not just Biblical, it is legal. In other parts of the world, it is not. How beautiful it would be if some pediatricians there, even just a handful, were to hear a gentle call of the Lord to work to help reduce the incidence of abuse in our world of today.

Gender Ideology

There is much confusion surrounding gender identity. Some call it the time of a "gender revolution" where even young children, years away from puberty, can choose their gender independent of their sexual identity. Unfortunately, some pediatricians are fully supportive of the gender revolution and actively promote it. Others, maybe many of the majority, may sit passively by watching the events unfold. The pressure from a politically correct world can be a little overwhelming. There is more to the gender revolution than meets the eye. Not all medically presented data are really scientific - it can often have its own ideological bent, and there is still a great deal to be learned about the medical and psychological basis for gender confusion.

Various documents in the Church make reference to gender issues and knowing what has been said can be helpful for pediatricians grappling with these issues in their practice. The Pontifical Council for the Family stated:

> Starting from the decade between 1960-1970, some theories ... hold not only that generic sexual identity ("gender") is the product of an interaction between the community and the individual, but that this generic identity is independent from personal sexual identity: i.e. that masculine and feminine genders in society are the exclusive product of social factors, with no relation to any truth about the sexual dimension of the person. In this way, any sexual attitude can be justified, including homosexuality, and it is society that ought to change in order to include other genders, together with male and female, in its way of shaping social life. (Pontifical Council for the Family 2000, n. 8)

The Congregation for the Doctrine of the Faith, in a letter to the Bishops of the Catholic Church in 2004, stated "In this perspective, physical difference, termed sex, is minimized, while the purely cultural element, termed gender, is emphasized to the maxi- mum and held to be primary." (Congregation for the Doctrine of the Faith 2004, n. 2)

Most Catholics have no idea that Pope Francis has spoken out and also written many times and on various occasions about the issue of gender ideology. For example, on an apostolic journey to Poland in 2016 he said:

> In Europe, America, Latin America, Africa, and in some countries of Asia, there are genuine forms of ideological colonization taking place. And one of these - I will call it clearly by its name - is [the ideology of] "gender." Today children - children! - are taught in school that everyone can choose his or her sex. Why are they teaching this? Because the books are provided by the persons and institutions that give you money. These forms of ideological colonization are also supported by influential countries. And this terrible! (Francis 2016b)

In *Laudato Si'* we find

> valuing one's own body in its femininity or masculinity is necessary if I am going to be able to recognize myself in an encounter with someone who is different. In this way we can joyfully accept the specific gifts of another man or woman, the work of God the Creator, and find mutual enrichment. It is not a healthy attitude which would seek "to cancel out sexual difference because it no longer knows how to confront it." (Francis 2015, n. 155)

And in *Amoris Laetitia*, Pope Francis (2016a) notes

Yet another challenge is posed by the various forms of an ideology of gender that "denies the difference and reciprocity in nature of a man and a woman and envisages a society without sexual differences, thereby eliminating the anthropological basis of the family. This ideology leads to educational programmes and legislative enactments that promote a personal identity and emotional intimacy radically separated from the biological difference between male and female. Consequently, human identity becomes the choice of the individual, one which can also change over time." It is a source of concern that some ideologies of this sort, which seek to respond to what are at times understandable aspirations, manage to assert themselves as absolute and unquestionable, even dictating how children should be raised. It needs to be emphasized that "biological sex and the socio-cultural role of sex (gender) can be distinguished but not separated." (n. 56)

A recent document from the Congregation for Catholic Education (2019) entitled "'Male and female he created them' - towards a path of dialogue on the question of gender theory in education" notes that "it is becoming increasingly clear that we are now facing with what might accurately be called an educational crisis, especially in the field of affectivity and sexuality" (n. 1). The document proposes a three-step process to correct aberrant theories regarding gender - listening, reasoning and proposing (Congregation for Catholic Education 2019). The importance of pedagogy is also emphasized, and a Catholic pediatrician is also a pedagogue - capable of guiding and positively influencing others.

It is therefore encouraging to see groups of pediatricians speaking out vocally against gender ideology. In a statement entitled "Gender Ideology Harms Children" updated in September 2017, the American College of Pediatricians (2017) made the following points:[1]

1. People who identify as "feeling like the opposite sex" or "somewhere in between" do not comprise a third sex. They remain biological men or biological women.

2. When an otherwise healthy biological boy believes he is a girl, or an otherwise healthy biological girl believes she is a boy, an objective psychological problem exists that lies in the mind not the body, and it should be treated as such. These children suffer from gender dysphoria. Gender dysphoria (GD), formerly listed as Gender Identity Disorder (GID), is a recognized mental disorder in the most recent edition of the Diagnostic and Statistical Manual of the American Psychiatric Association (DSM-5).

3. According to the DSM-5, as many as 98% of gender confused boys and 88% of gender confused girls eventually accept their biological sex after naturally passing through puberty.

4. Pre-pubertal children diagnosed with gender dysphoria may be given puberty blockers as young as eleven, and will require cross-sex hormones in later adolescence to continue impersonating the opposite sex.

5. Rates of suicide are nearly twenty times greater among adults who use cross-sex hormones and undergo sex reassignment surgery, even in Sweden which is among the most LGBTQ - affirming countries.

6. Conditioning children into believing a lifetime of chemical and surgical impersonation of the opposite sex is normal and healthful is child abuse.

How I wish I could hear a pediatric voice of reason (and science) resound more loudly on gender issues in medical, legal, and scientific circles, and in the secular media.[2]

Abortion

Annually there are an estimated 75 million abortions each year worldwide. In front of the massive loss of life, how can a Catholic pediatrician be silent? It would be a sin of grave omission. One cannot be excused by claiming that "it is not my specialty." That could be quite a lame excuse and will hold little water on the day of judgment! Claiming as a Catholic pediatrician that abortion is not their concern is akin to Pilate washing his hands trying to absolve himself from being responsible for the death of Christ. Our Lord even said "Amen, I say to you, what you did not do for one of these least ones, you did not do for me" (Matt 25:45).

Pope Francis (2016a) speaks so clearly on the wrongs of abortion.

> Here I feel it urgent to state that, if the family is the sanctuary of life, the place where life is conceived and cared for, it is a horrendous contradiction when it becomes a place where life is rejected and destroyed. So great is the value of a human life, and so inalienable the right to life of an innocent child growing in the mother's womb, that no alleged right to one's own body can justify a decision to terminate that life, which is an end in itself and which can never be considered the "property" of another human being. (n. 83)

Mother Teresa was also a vocal critic of abortion. She spoke against the evils of abortion so courageously on various and prominent occasions. In her acceptance speech having received the Nobel Peace Prize in 1979, she made the following remarks.

> In the newspapers you read numbers of this one and that one being killed, this being destroyed, but nobody speaks of the millions of little ones who have been conceived to the same life as you and I, to the life of God, and we say nothing, we allow it. To me the nations who have legalized abortion, they are the poorest nations. They are afraid of the little one, they are afraid of the unborn child, and the child must die because they don't want to feed one more child, to educate one more child, the child

The Pediatrician as Prophet

> must die ... today, I ask His Majesties here before you all who come from different countries, let us all pray that we have the courage to stand by the unborn child, and give the child an opportunity to love and to be loved, and I think with God's grace we will be able to bring peace in the world. (Mother Teresa 1979)

At the National Prayer Breakfast in Washington, DC, on February 5, 1994, she addressed the high-powered audience on the wrongs of abortion.

> I feel that the greatest destroyer of peace today is abortion, because it is a war against the child, a direct killing of the innocent child, murder by the mother herself. And if we accept that a mother can kill even her own child, how can we tell other people not to kill one another? How do we persuade a woman not to have an abortion? As always, we must persuade her with love and we remind ourselves that love means to be willing to give until it hurts. Jesus gave even His life to love us. So, the mother who is thinking of abortion, should be helped to love, that is, to give until it hurts her plans, or her free time, to respect the life of her child. The father of that child, whoever he is, must also give until it hurts.

> By abortion, the mother does not learn to love, but kills even her own child to solve her problems. And, by abortion, that father is told

> that he does not have to take any responsibility at all for the child he has brought into the world. The father is likely to put other women into the same trouble. So abortion just leads to more abortion. Any country that accepts abortion is not teaching its people to love, but to use any violence to get what they want. This is why the greatest destroyer of love and peace is abortion. (Mother Teresa 1994a).

Later that year, in a statement sent to the Cairo International Conference on Population and Development (September 9, 1994), she made the following remarks.

> I have said often, and I am sure of it, that the greatest destroyer of peace in the world today is abortion. If a mother can kill her own child, what is there to stop you and me from killing each other? The only one who has the right to take life is the One who has created it. Nobody else has that right: not conference, no government. I am sure that deep down in your heart, you know that the unborn child is a human being loved by God, like you and me. How can anyone knowing that, deliberately destroy that life? It frightens me to think of all the people who kill their conscience so that they can perform an abortion. When we die, we will come face to face with God, the Author of life. Who will give an account to God for the millions and millions of babies who were not

allowed to have the chance to live, to experience loving and being loved?

God has created a world big enough for all the lives He wishes to be born. It is only our hearts that are not big enough to want them and accept them. If all the money that is being spent on finding ways to kill people was used instead to feed them and house them and educate them - how beautiful that would be. We are too often afraid of the sacrifices we might have to make. But where there is love, there is always sacrifice. And when we love until it hurts, there is joy and peace.

If there is a child that you don't want or can't feed or educate, give that child to me. I will not refuse any child. I will give a home, or find loving parents for him or for her. We are fighting abortion by adoption and have given thousands of children to caring families. And it is so beautiful to see the love and unity that a child brings to a family. (Mother Teresa 1994b)

She repeated her strong condemnation of abortion in 1995, in a written message to the Fourth World Conference on Women, sponsored by the United Nations in Beijing, China.

That special power of loving that belongs to a woman is seen most clearly when she becomes a mother. Motherhood is the gift of God to women. How grateful we must be to God for this wonderful gift that brings such joy to the whole world, women and men alike! Yet we can destroy this gift of motherhood, especially by the evil of abortion, but also be thinking that other things like jobs or positions are more important than loving, than giving oneself to others. (Mother Teresa 1995)

Mother Teresa always used these moments on the world stage to speak out strongly in defense of life. Pediatricians are also invited to so many conferences worldwide. How wonderful if they also used these opportunities not only to present papers and receive more accolades but also, even in some small way, to be faithful to their prophetic task. Perhaps as doctors we can all ask ourselves, in what way have I helped stand up for the rights of the unborn child? Am I willing to sacrifice, even a little, my image, to swallow my pride, to risk even a little my reputation in speaking out against the injustice of killing of the innocent life in the womb? Or will we continue to keep quiet? Saint Mother Teresa intercede for us!

IVF

It is not unlikely that pediatricians might come across infertile couples seeking recourse to IVF. It is clear that IVF results in a massive destruction of human embryonic life. The number of embryos sacrificed, even in the most technically advanced centers of artificial fertilization, hovers above 80% (Congregation for the Doctrine of the Faith 2008, footnote 27). This is to say nothing about the over 1 million embryos cryogenically preserved in liquid nitrogen.

Knowing clearly the Church teaching that life begins at conception, we cannot be content or at peace seeing the nascent embryonic life treated in this way. Now again one may try to claim a kind of "diplomatic immunity" and excuse oneself from the evangelizing duty by stating that as a pediatrician in the hospital or clinic one does not generally encounter this reality of infertility and requests for IVF.

Can we not say how shallow this type of reasoning is? One is not only a Catholic doctor when in the clinic but also when outside in the world of today. Even as a surgeon, the topic of IVF came up in conversations with my friends, at dinner parties, and in situations of everyday life. These are all opportunities to gently inform others of the soundness of Catholic Church teaching and why she says "no" to IVF.

Her reasons to say "no" can be summarized as follows: the IVF process causes a massive destruction of human embryonic life, the child comes to be treated not as a gift but as a manufacturing product, and in the IVF process, the unitive and procreative dimensions of the marital act are separated. Specific Church teaching on reproductive technologies and IVF can be found in her documents *Donum vitae* and *Dignitas personae* (Congregation for the Doctrine of the Faith, 1987).

JESUS THE DIVINE PHYSICIAN

Pediatric Euthanasia

The commandment "Do not kill" clearly reminds us of our responsibility to take care of life. Most people of good will hold that the doctors' task is to save, defend, and uphold life. Perhaps they would be staggered to find a rapidly growing movement within the medical profession itself increasingly in favor of euthanasia and physician-assisted suicide. This not only takes place in adults. The Groningen Protocol, reported in the *New England Journal of Medicine*, chillingly states the various conditions required to actively end the life of a suffering newborn. Not only Holland, but Belgium, whose population is three-quarters Catholic, also allows euthanasia of children. This is one area in which pediatricians cannot claim immunity: this touches their patients directly and they cannot be silent.

How to Exercise the Prophetic Task?

Not all advocacy is confined to legislative lobbying or to influencing the position of one's own hospital, practice, or professional organization. Perhaps the most important way of changing the world is just as Jesus taught us: one person at a time in the situations we are presented in life.

- When these issues arise at dinner or in conversations with other doctors, the Catholic position can be gently but clearly underlined and explained. If a new issue comes up, we can take note and later read up about so we will be better prepared next time to respond.

- The use of social media is increasingly important, especially in influencing the young. Many now use Twitter to share Catholic teaching on life issues. Others write in blogs and Facebook to defend life.

- Keeping track of world events such as the Ireland abortion referendum and using them as a gateway to witness, to "give reasons for our faith" (see 1 Pet 3:15).

- Being updated on Church pronouncements on topical issues such as gender confusion, you can perhaps add this task to the busy workload of your Catholic guild chaplain or parish priest. Another good source is your friendly neighborhood moral theologian (who views are consonant with Catholic Church teaching) or keeping up to date with the contents of a reputable Catholic journal of medical ethics/bioethics.

- Relevant issues can be mentioned in talks at medical case conferences or discussions and the Catholic position presented.

- Highlighting advocacy themes in talks not only at Catholic but also at secular medical conferences. It does not always require an explicit faith reference, after all we are advised at times to be "as cunning as snakes and as innocent as doves" (Matthew 10:16). Themes such as justice or equality, which are firmly grounded in Catholic social teaching, are themes of universal appeal.

- Looking out for opportunities to publish on advocacy themes in medical or ethical journals. Letters can be written to the editor of the local newspaper or the parish bulletin on pertinent medical issues of interest.

Love for Christ and Catholic church teaching will help us to be creative in looking for ways to stand up for life knowing that "the true apostle is on the lookout for occasions to announce Christ" (Catechism of the Catholic Church 1997, n. 905).

Conclusion

One thing is for sure - we cannot afford to sit by and watch idly. That is why I wrote this article and that is why I try to be active as a priest (and a medical doctor) in areas of advocacy. Sometimes the task at hand can seem overwhelming as if the odds are stacked against us, as if it is a lost cause, quite hopeless, and not worth embarking on. We can be men and women of little faith! Like the apostles, we have to have beg "Lord increase our faith" (Lk 17:5). The call is to not lose confidence but continue sowing the seed through sharing our words and opinions, to believe that even consciences that seem dead can come back to life.

At times, the problems can seem too big. Perhaps the prophet Ezekiel felt similarly challenged when God showed him a vision of a valley full of dry bones. God asked him "Son of man, can these bones come to life?" (Ez 37:1-14). Quite humbly, Ezekiel replies "Lord God, you alone know that." The Lord then said to Ezekiel "Prophesy over these bones, and say to them: Dry bones, hear the word of the Lord! Thus says the Lord God to these bones: See! I will bring spirit into you, that you may come to life. I will put sinews upon you, make flesh grow over you, cover you with skin, and put spirit in you so that you may come to life and know that I am the Lord."

Ezekiel has faith in what the Lord was telling him and was obedient. The Word of God recounts "I prophesied as I had been told, and even as I was prophesying I heard a noise; it was a rattling as the bones came together, bone joining bone."

If each one of us reading this is "faithful in small" (Matt 25:21) perhaps we too can be surprised like Ezekiel was. We too can witness many dry bones coming to life and many consciences regaining sensitivity to life. I pray for the witness and advocacy of many Catholic pediatricians. May your voices be heard and may the words of St Catherine of Siena move us to action "Speak the truth with a thousand voices, because it is silence that makes the world go rotten."

Notes

1. This statement is critiqued by David Albert Jones (2017), the director of the Anscombe Bioethics Centre in Oxford, United Kingdom, in an article entitled "The American College of Pediatricians Statement on "Gender Ideology": A Note of Caution" published in the *Catholic Medical Quarterly*, the journal of the Catholic Medical Association in the United Kingdom.

However, Adrian Treloar (2017) then expresses concern regarding the views of David Albert Jones in a subsequent correspondence with the same journal.

2. Many today in the Philippines are pushing for the passage of the so-called sexual orientation or gender identity (SOGI) bill 4982. While there may be many laudable parts, I am surprised at how some statements pass so easily and go unchallenged such as "A person may have a male or female identity with the physiological characteristics of the opposite sex, in which case the person is considered transgender." Or again "Sex refers to male, female, or intersex. Intersex refers to people born with the sex characteristics (including genitals, gonads and chromosome patterns) that do not fit typical binary notions of male and female bodies, all of which are natural bodily variations along a spectrum." Quite frankly some of the statements in the bill are verging on pseudo-science. It would be beautiful to hear a more definitive voice from Catholic pediatricians here, to give some light amidst the seeming confusion in the area of sexual identity and gender issues.

References

American College of Pediatricians. 2017. "Gender Ideology Harms Children."

Boursiquot, Marie-Alberte. 2017. "Letter of the President to CMA Colleagues and Members (January 10). Cameleon in the Philippines."

Catechism of the Catholic Church. 1997. 2nd ed. Vatican City: Libreria Editrice Vaticana.

Code of Canon Law. 1983.

Congregation for Catholic Education. 2019. "Male and Female He Created Them" towards A Path of Dialogue on the Question of Gender Theory in Education.

Congregation for the Doctrine of the Faith. 1987. *Donum Vitae.*

Congregation for the Doctrine of the Faith. 2004. *Letter to the Bishops of the Catholic Church on the Collaboration of Men and Women in the Church and in the World.*

Congregation for the Doctrine of the Faith. 2008. *Dignitas Personae.*

Council for the Welfare of Children and UNICEF. 2016. "National Baseline Study on Violence against Children: Philippines." Executive Summary, October.

Francis, Pope. 2013. *Evangelii Gaudium.*

Francis, Pope. 2015. *Laudato Si'.*

Francis, Pope. 2016a. *Amoris Laetitia.*

Francis, Pope. 2016b. "Address to Meeting of Polish Bishops." *Cathedral of Kraków*, July 27.

John Paul II, Pope. 1988. *Christifideles Laici.*

Jones, David Albert. 2017. "The American College of Pediatricians Statement on 'Gender Ideology': A Note of Caution." *Catholic Medical Quarterly* 67:11-14.

Mother Teresa. 1979. "Acceptance Speech Having Received the Nobel Peace Prize." University of Oslo, Norway, December 10.

Mother Teresa. 1994a. "Speech at National Prayer Breakfast in Washington, D.C, USA." February 5.

Mother Teresa. 1994b. "Statement for the Cairo International Conference on Population and Development." September 9.

Mother Teresa. 1995. "Written Message to the Fourth World Conference on Women in Beijing, China. September 12.

Paul, VI, Pope. 1975. *Evangelii Nuntiandi.*

Pontifical Council for the Family. 2000. *Family, Marriage and "De Facto" Unions.*

Ramiro, Laurie S., Bernadette J. Madrid, and David W. Brown. 2010. "Adverse Childhood Experiences (ACE) and Health-risk Behaviors among Adults in a Developing Country Setting." *Child Abuse & Neglect* 34:842-55.

Treloar, Adrian. 2017. "The American College of Pediatricians: Statement on 'Gender Ideology': A Note of Caution." *Catholic Medical Quarterly* 67.

Vatican Council II. 1964. *Lumen Gentium.*

DECISION MAKING IN NEONATAL END-OF-LIFE SCENARIOS IN LOW-INCOME SETTINGS[1]

Summary

The challenge of decision making in end-of-life scenarios is exacerbated when the patient is a newborn and in a low-income setting. The principle of proportionate care is a helpful guide but needs to be applied. The complex interplay of benefit, burden, and cost of various treatments all need to be considered. In patients with severe neonatal encephalopathy, prognosis can be hard to determine, and a team approach to decision making can help. In low-income settings, or where there are limited resources, the ideal care needs to be incarnated in the real context. Issues of social justice also arise as finite resources need to be used prudently.

Decision making in end-of-life scenarios can be difficult. When a loved one is sick and emotions are running high, families can be physically tired, and clinical outcomes are not always predictable. A helpful ethical principle for decision making at the end of life is that of proportionate means.

AVOIDING EXTREMES: THE PRINCIPLE OF PROPORTIONATE MEANS

In the *Ethical and Religious Directives for Catholic Health Care Services* we find:

> A person has a moral obligation to use ordinary or proportionate means of pre- serving his or her life. Proportionate means are those that in the judgment of the patient offer a reasonable hope of benefit and do not entail an excessive burden or impose excessive expense on the family or the community.
>
> A person may forgo extraordinary or disproportionate means of preserving life. Disproportionate means are those that in the patient's judgment do not offer a reasonable hope of benefit or entail an excessive burden, or impose excessive expense on the family or the community. (USCCB 2009, dirs. 56-57)

Using this principle, we hope to avoid two obvious extremes: on the one hand euthanasia[2] and on the other therapeutic obstinacy or futile care where instead of helping one simply prolongs the dying process. One has to carefully navigate the good ship "patient care" between these two extremes. It is interesting to note that it is often "easier" to continue support, even if it prolongs the dying process and is actually "futile," than to discontinue disproportionate means when death may be the result.

Aristotle's so-called doctrine of the mean also may come in handy. He introduces it in his *Nicomachean Ethics*, and it has become a key tenet of virtue ethics. The doctrine of the mean avoids the extremes, called vices: one set of "vices" to avoid here are euthanasia on the one hand and over-aggressive or futile care on the other. The medical team and family instead seek to follow the virtuous middle path. This is not an arithmetical mean, but rather a carefully judged response to the concrete situation at hand. Considering the cost of treatment proposed, it may not mean to pay zero and withdraw all financial support, or to spend $10,000 (which, if grossly excessive, may be a vice). The doctrine of the mean does not result in a proposal to spend $5,000 (the arithmetical mean), but in a given context to spend $1,000 and in another $8,000. It leads one to make a reasoned judgment on the matter of how much to spend in the particular circumstances. Aristotle suggests that we should consider questions such as: is this the right time, about the right things, toward the right people, for the right end, and in the right way? (Aristotle 1953, bk. 2, chap. 6 [1106b]).

THE ROLE OF THE CONSCIENCE

Aristotle noted that vice can obscure our moral vision (Aristotle 1953, bk. 6, chap. 12 [1144a]).[3] Vice could be understood at various levels:

- At the level of society, when legislators actively push for euthanasia legislation as is happening in Canada and various countries now;

- At the level of the hospital, which, seeking to maximize profits, too easily proposes treatments that may not be strictly medically necessary;

- At the level of the doctor, who, influenced by favors received from pharmaceutical companies, too readily prescribes their treatments/products;

- At the level of the family, who, experiencing emotions unbridled by reason, insist that "everything be done" even if the treatment would cause harm.

The locus of decision making, where the doctrine of the mean is worked out, extremes avoided, and the virtuous path sought, is the conscience. Catholic moral theology acknowledges the vital role our conscience plays in decision making.

The *Catechism of the Catholic Church* notes:

> Conscience is a judgment of reason whereby the human person recognizes the moral quality of a concrete act that he is going to perform, is in the process of performing, or has already completed. (Catechism 1997, n. 1778)

> Conscience includes the perception of the principles of morality (synderesis); their application in the given circumstances by practical discernment of reasons and goods. (Catechism 1997, n. 1780)

A well-formed conscience can assist medical decision making. In my experience many doctors are unfamiliar with the principle of proportionate means and often experience hesitation and uncertainty when dealing with end-of-life decisions.

Decision Making in Neonatal End-of-life Scenarios in Low-income Settings

THE PARTICULAR CASE OF THE GRAVELY ILL NEWBORN

St Alphonsus Liguori, the Catholic patron saint of moral theology, wrote about the challenge of applying moral principles to particular cases. In one moment, he explained the task of the confessor, stating that the confessor has the role of a doctor of the soul; to identify the spiritual sickness of the person and prescribe the treatment. "Who would deny that all cases have to be resolved with principles? But herein lies the difficulty: to apply to particular cases the principles appropriate to them" (Liguori 1755, n. 17).[4] The doctor at the bedside is similarly faced with the challenging task of applying to a particular case, the relevant medical principles. How to apply the (general) principle of proportionate means to this patient (particular case) in front of me?

Perhaps the usual ethical and clinical context for the application of the principle of proportionate means is in elderly patients nearing the end of their lives (or acutely ill adults in grave condition). The situation is exacerbated when the patient is a newborn as we presume they would have more years of life ahead of them. It is one thing is to apply the principle when the patient is 90 years old, but what if they are just 9 days old or 9 hours old? I would like to apply the principle of proportionate means to critically ill neonates in end-of-life scenarios. When specificity is needed by way of highlighting a point, I will refer to the condition of neonatal encephalopathy, a "major contributor to global childhood mortality and morbidity" (Wilkinson

2010, e451). Applying the principle of proportionate means, I will consider the aspect of benefit, burden, and cost in determining whether to pursue a given line of treatment or not in a critically ill neonate.[5]

The clinical report on "Hypothermia and Neonatal Encephalopathy" from the American Academy of Pediatrics indicates the type of gold standard care an infant with hypoxic-ischemic encephalopathy can expect:

> Medical centers offering hypothermia should be capable of providing comprehensive clinical care, including mechanical ventilation; physiologic (vital signs, temperature) and biochemical (blood gas) monitoring; neuroimaging, including MRI; seizure detection and monitoring with aEEG or EEG; neurologic consultation; and a system in place for monitoring longitudinal neurodevelopmental outcome. (American Academy of Pediatrics 2014, 1149)[6]

With such a gamut of treatments, how is one to assess "benefit" and "burden" in an infant of a few days old? Primarily one could consider the burden to the infant and also the burden to the family, and perhaps even to the society. With complex treatment paths, should one take each modality one by one, such as burden of ventilation, burden of hypothermia, and so on, and then do a kind of summation?[7] Here the Church offers helpful advice on how to proceed, listing various elements of treatment planning and suggesting to evaluate

> the type of treatment to be used, its degree of complexity or risk, its cost and the possibilities of using it, and comparing these elements with the result that can be expected, taking into account the state of the sick person and his or her physical and moral resources. (CDF 1980, part IV)

Usually, a doctor in practice would consider the collective burden of the whole treatment package and, if funds are lacking, may be able to offer a tailored package such that vital treatments can be sustained and subsidiary ones omitted.

Complex questions may include how to assess the "burden" of a future disability. The child may not be able to express a verbal opinion and the assessment would fall on the parents and carers.[8] Many times this child, with concomitant disabilities, is considered a real blessing by their families. However there also exist unfortunate scenarios where the carers are left unsupported - with minimal assistance to help ease their heavy burden of care.

Cost and financial limitations

The consideration of cost becomes especially problematic in low-income countries where often the financial burden of health care falls largely on patients and their family.[9] Some examples can help further situate a reader who is not familiar with the challenge of offering good neonatal care in a developing world context.

- In the Philippines, full supportive care and ventilation of a neonate costs approximately $200 per *day* in a government hospital. This can pose a tremendous financial strain on families where the usual *monthly* wage is only US $300.[10]

- Here in a government neonatal unit in the Philippines, there are many who qualify as "charity patients" - those who belong to a poor family and thus do not have to pay for the hospital stay, any operation costs or doctors' fees. The family only has to pay for medicines and/or additional treatments such as surfactant. When the premature child needs surfactant (usually one vial would suffice, or at most two) the cost is 20,000 Philippine pesos (approximately $400). If they cannot afford this, the child usually will spend longer on the ventilator or does not survive.

- When a child needs ventilation, it can be provided for free to a charity case. However, the parents still need to buy the necessary tubing to allow their child to be connected to the ventilator. The tubing costs $60 - $80. Until they find this money, the family or relatives will have to handbag the baby. The hand bagging may last for a few hours to more than 24 hours, until the funds are found.

- For babies with hydrocephalus, ideally a CT (computerized tomography) scan would be performed post-delivery and a ventriculo-peritoneal (VP) shunt eventually placed to drain excess fluid from the ventricles of the brain. Here the parents will have to find the money for both the CT scan (around $100) and the VP shunt (around $300). Often it takes some two weeks or more before the CT scan is performed and many more weeks for surgery. While the parents look for funding, frequently, the baby will become sick.

In these and many other similar situations of scarcity, unable to afford the "gold standard" care, the family and attending medical team sadly, but realistically, may have to settle for silver or bronze.

Decisions and prognosis

Decisions based on foreseeable benefit are difficult because outcomes may be unpredictable: "The major problem that confronts those caring for infants who have hypoxic-ischemic encephalopathy is how to provide families with reliable information about outcome. ... The difficulty lies in how long to pursue treatment in infants who may have a very poor prognosis" (Allan 2002, e108).

It may be difficult in the period of initial injury to give clear information regarding prognosis but as "the neonatal illness progresses over the first few days, more information becomes available, and the accuracy of prediction of outcome of survivors improves" (Robertson and Perlman 2006, 279).

Magnetic resonance imaging (MRI) is often used to provide prognostic information in severe hypoxic-ischemic encephalopathy but its overall usefulness and reliability remains to be fully ascertained (Wilkinson 2010).

Where health resources are not readily available, it may not be possible to perform MRI scans or do an EEG to confirm brain activity or death. Here the medical team can rely only on a clinical judgment of brain death.[11] At times mechanical ventilation and full support may be continued in a brain-dead infant seemingly in direct contradiction to the principle of proportionate means. One reason for this is that the parents may not be able to accept immediately the death of their beloved newborn and the support is continued to allow a few more days to allow the parents more time to take in the situation and to grieve. In the Philippines it is common for one parent to be working overseas. More time may be needed to allow them to arrive before disconnecting the ventilator. The continued ventilation and support of a braindead baby may be judged "disproportionate," but disproportionate treatments are optional, and some circumstances such as the aforementioned, may indicate their continuation for a short period of time.

Doctors also may feel uncomfortable when confronted with end-of-life dilemmas for a variety of reasons. Gloth observes that "without formal training, physicians can feel impotent in addressing the palliative needs of end-stage patients" (Gloth 2011, 75). Perhaps the training in medical school was lacking, or simply was more technical than ethical, such that the doctor later feels insecure and hesitant in addressing any moral conundrums.

Decision Making in Neonatal End-of-life Scenarios in Low-income Settings

At times the medical situation is not ideal: doctors may wish to prescribe a certain treatment according to their training or in line with the latest recommendations from developed world settings. A doctor can be inspired reading the latest guidelines on end-of-life issues from a highly specialized palliative care unit overseas, but in her setting, she may have difficulty to put the guidelines in practice. Here in the Philippines, there are no palliative care units, only a palliative care service. Sometimes the ideal treatment is unavailable, or if it is available, it might be unaffordable to the family. The doctor may face a dilemma of conscience knowing what he or she could do in an ideal situation but facing real-world limits. There is an obvious tension here between what the doctor would like to do and what he or she can actually do in practice.

This tension can weigh heavy on the doctor's conscience but he or she can be reassured and encouraged to do the best in the given situation: the moral judgment regarding a particular medical case always needs to be incarnated in the actual context. As Pope Francis noted "There also exists a constant tension between ideas and realities. Realities simply are, whereas ideas are worked out. There has to be continuous dialogue between the two, lest ideas become detached from realities" (Francis 2013, n. 231).

Additionally, there may exist a grey zone in which the proper course of treatment is uncertain. In some situations, treatment is clearly to be pursued, and in others, clearly wrong. In between there exists a grey zone. In these situations, time may be helpful. The neonatal ICU could be offered for a fixed time, such as one week, to allow the progress of the child to be more carefully assessed. However, where limited resources exist, one may be forced to make premature medical decisions with greater uncertainty. In general families can be encouraged to do what they can.

Breaking the news

Various hospital groups, such as the Queensland Maternity and Neonatal Program, have clinical guidelines, which include advice that can be given to parents when discussing aspects of hypoxic-ischemic encephalopathy (see Table 1 on next page; Queensland Department of Health 2016, 20).

The Royal Children's Hospital in Victoria, Australia, has produced a handbook called *Caring Decisions* to assist parents facing end-of-life decisions for their child (Wilkinson et al. n.d.). In front of the decision to "Do not attempt resuscitation" (DNAR) the parents may ask, "Will I be a bad parent if I agree to a DNAR order for my child?" The response in *Caring Decisions* is "No. If life support is not helpful, or will do more harm than good, the best and most loving decision is to make sure that a child is kept comfortable" (Wilkinson et al. n.d., 12).

Decision Making in Neonatal End-of-life Scenarios in Low-income Settings

Table 1   Hypoxic-ischaemic encephalopathy

Incidence	About 1-4 in 1000 newborn babies suffer from the effects of reduced blood flow or oxygen supply to their brain around the time of birth.
Consequences	This can result in brain damage from direct injury and also from subsequent secondary changes within the brain.
	These secondary changes are known to increase the amount of brain injury that occurs. Within 6 hours from injury there is a chance to lessen the secondary changes.
Prognosis	Babies with mild brain injury often have a normal outcome.
	Approximately 30 to 60 percent of those babies who survive after more severe damage to their brain may develop long-term disabilities. These disabilities include cerebral palsy and severe learning difficulties.

Feelings of guilt

Feelings of guilt are commonly observed in families with a sick newborn. Some feel they did something wrong or that they should be doing more. This can lead to insistence on providing over-aggressive, disproportionate means.

Doctors should try to understand the dilemma of the family but avoid being bullied also. The authors of *Caring Decisions* note,

> Sometimes when doctors talk to families about life support treatment, parents reply that they want 'everything done.' It is natural to feel this way. The doctors and nurses will do everything they can to help your child. But some treatments are not helpful. It is really important that doctors avoid doing things that would harm your child (Wilkinson et al. n.d., 13).

When treatment needs to be discontinued, the family should be supported through the process, and helped to understand that the most caring decision might be to "let their loved one go." They can be comforted in this difficult moment by the objective teaching of the Church: "Discontinuing medical procedures that are burdensome, dangerous, extraordinary, or disproportionate to the expected outcome can be legitimate; it is the refusal of 'over-zealous' treatment. Here one does not will to cause death; one's inability to impede it is merely accepted" (Catechism 1997, n. 2278).

Feelings of guilt may also be found among doctors. At times doctors themselves can be confused and unclear of the difference between withdrawing disproportionate treatment and euthanasia. In *Evangelium vitae*, Pope John Paul II explained

Decision Making in Neonatal End-of-life Scenarios in Low-income Settings

> Euthanasia must be distinguished from the decision to forego so-called "aggressive medical treatment," in other words, medical procedures that no longer correspond to the real situation of the patient, either because they are by now disproportionate to any expected results or because they impose an excessive burden on the patient and his family. It needs to be determined whether the means of treatment available are objectively proportionate to the prospects for improvement. To forego extraordinary or disproportionate means is not the equivalent of suicide or euthanasia; it rather expresses acceptance of the human condition in the face of death. (John Paul 1995, n. 65)[12]

It can also help if delicate topics are addressed with time, not waiting for catastrophic moments to begin the sensitive dialogue, but foreseeing and actively anticipating the need. In this way parents, and relatives, have time to assimilate the gravity of the situation. Multi-disciplinary dialogues, in the form of case conferences, are helpful, where the family can meet and discuss their child's care with representatives of the various teams involved, including doctors, nurses, speech therapy, physiotherapy, and the like. The presence of a person from the hospital bioethics committee and a religious representative such as a priest may also be indicated. At times, difficult decisions can be confronted more readily through a team approach.

Preferential option for the poor and social justice

One important principle from Catholic social teaching is the so-called "preferential option for the poor." Pope John Paul II described it as "an option, or a special form of primacy in the exercise of Christian charity, to which the whole tradition of the Church bears witness" (John Paul II 1987, n. 42). This challenges us to give a preferential consideration to the poor and those "without medical care" (John Paul II 1987, n. 42). Pope Francis in *Amoris Laetitia*, his recent exhortation on love in the family, also calls our attention to those who suffer because of a lack of access to "adequate health care" (Francis 2016, n. 44). Living out this preferential option for the poor, many doctors here in the Philippines admirably attempt to raise funds to help pay for the medicines and hospital bills of their poor patients. They offer not only part of their "spare time" to do this (up to half a day's work for certain patients) but even a part of their own salary in the search for everything from donor breast milk, diapers, examinations, tests, even up to life saving equipment.

The Catholic bishops of the Philippines remind us of the social aspect of justice in health care. In number 1039 of the *Catechism for Filipino Catholics* we hear,

> However, when there is no real hope for the patient's genuine benefit, there is no moral obligation to prolong life artificially by the use of various drugs and machines. In fact, using extraordinary means to keep comatose or terminally ill patients artificially alive seems

clearly to lack objective moral validity, especially in a society where the majority of the population do not enjoy even adequate elementary health care. (Catechism for Filipino Catholics 1997, n. 1039)

In the setting of a government hospital here in the Philippines, many patients are provided care by the hospital's social services. In needlessly pursuing disproportionate means, families may not only be draining their own limited resources, but that of the hospital as well - which resources could instead be used to benefit other charity patients in need. Charles C. Camosy nicely summarizes the interplay of responsibilities telling us that all persons "have a right to a proportionate amount of the community's resources - and a duty to refrain from using a disproportionate amount" (Camosy 2010, 92).

Overview of scenarios

It is not possible to present the varied and multiform clinical situations one may encounter in a child with hypoxic-ischemic encephalopathy. However, before we wrap up our discussion, it may be beneficial to present some paradigmatic scenarios amidst a myriad of clinical possibilities. The following situations are by no means exhaustive but may be helpful as reference points. For each scenario a brief course of action is suggested.

- The child is treatable and the family can afford the treatment. Here the choice is obvious to offer the treatment so that the child can recover.

- The family has a limited budget so treatment should be tailored to match their resources. The situation here is more difficult, and needs to take into account the prognosis, resources available, and the possibility of obtaining additional resources. Spiritual and ethical guidance, for example from a priest, may be particularly helpful in this situation to both guide the family to an ethical decision and lessen any guilt they may feel from being unable to afford the highest level of care.[13]

- Severe brain injury with uncertain prognosis - here a limited time trial of treatment can be offered. When the moment of decision arrives one option may be to withdraw treatment (considered disproportionate) knowing the child's death will ensue.[14] At times it can be hard for the medical staff to confront the possibility of death (or even future serious disability) of a neonate and difficult to discuss these issues with the family members: "One difficulty a physician may face is broaching the topic of discontinuing care with the patient's family - in a sensitive manner that will not cause undue feelings of helplessness, anger or even indifference from the family."[15] Clinicians need to communicate the relevant information in a way that is open, honest, truthful, thoughtful, and compassionate.

- The child may recover but afterward have a severe cognitive and physical deficit. In low-income settings, the family can really struggle to care for such a child. Often supportive services such as physiotherapy or speech therapy may be sadly lacking or usually non-existent if the patient lives at any distance from the major hospitals. The saving grace in the Philippines is that families are often large and inter-generational, living under the same roof. At times the care is done by a sibling, relative, or even a neighbor, offering some respite to the primary carer.

- The parents may insist on treatment that the medical team considers disproportionate. The doctor may be constrained by limited resources and feel it wholly inappropriate to purse over-aggressive care in such a futile situation.

Where a strong and irreconcilable difference of opinion exists between the family and the medical team, and the situation cannot be resolved, transfer to an alternative hospital may have to be considered. However, this may be "a wholly unsatisfactory resolution since the ethical dilemma is not 'solved' by moving it to another location" (Linacre Institute 2007, 261).

Conclusion

At times decision making in medicine is challenging and complex, especially when the patient is newborn and the decision may mean life or death. The principle of proportionate means is helpful but it needs to be applied. In low-income settings not all prognostic data may be readily available.

Doctors have to strive nobly to do their best in limited situations. Having to keep in mind an ideal but live in the real world can be a source of tension in the carers.

Extremes should be avoided, and doctors should not be coerced into providing treatments that harm or prolong the burden. Where resources are limited, issues of social justice should be taken seriously.

Notes

1. A shorter version of this paper was delivered by the author at the 3rd international convention of the Philippine Society of Newborn Medicine, "Cutting Edge Neonatology: Applications in the Developing World," February 1-3, 2017, in Manila, Philippines.

2. The Groningen Protocol, reported in the New England Journal of Medicine, chillingly states the various conditions required to actively end the life of a suffering newborn. While such a protocol would clearly contravene the doctor's principle of "do no [further] harm," the authors do recognize that "discussions regarding the initiation and continuation of treatment in newborns with serious medical conditions are one of the most difficult aspects of pediatric practice" (Verhagen and Sauer 2005, 959). Presenting the position paper of the American College of Pediatricians, Vizcarrondo roundly critiques the Groningen Protocol stating, "Taking the suffering person's life is not the solution to the pain and suffering that are part of the dying process. The taking of innocent life is never a moral act. Neonatal euthanasia is not ethically permissible" (Vizcarrondo 2014, 392).

3. Thomson translates Aristotle here as "Now the supreme good appears such only to the good man, for vice gives a twist to our minds, making us hold false opinions about the principles of ethics" (Aristotle, trans. By Thomson 1953, 167-8).

4. My translation, from the Italian text "Chi niega che tutti i casi si hanno da risolvere coi principi? Ma qui sta la difficoltà: in applicare a' casi particolari i principi che loro convengono."

5. I have found the mnemonic "BBC" helpful to explain the main criteria of the principle of proportionate means when speaking to doctors and healthcare workers.

6. A plethora of literature exists in pediatric journals on the use of therapeutic hypothermia for hypoxic-ischemic encephalopathy. For low-income settings, the work of Shankaran (such as Pauliah et al. 2013), Galvao (Galvao et al. 2013), and Montaldo (Montaldo et al. 2015) is helpful. One challenge faced by doctors in poor countries is that to institute therapeutic hypothermia, prior blood-gas analysis is essential. However, blood-gas analysis machines are often scarce in low-income settings. In cases of neonatal hypoxic-ischemic encephalopathy, the gold standard care in a U.S. context for severely affected infants might consist of "mechanical ventilation, anticonvulsants, antibiotics, corticosteroids and pressor medications for blood pressure support, and IV fluids. Hypothermia for 72 hours (whole body cooling to ~93 degrees Fahrenheit) is now standard of care in the United

States. In the U.S., knowing the extent of brain damage and prognosticating about the associated outcomes require having access to MRI scanners to delineate the extent and severity of the brain damage. Sometimes the severely affected never recover the ability to be normal and need treatments like tracheostomy and gastric tube placement." Dr Tom Bender, Division of Medicine Neonatal-Perinatal Medicine, Department of Pediatrics, Saint Louis University School of Medicine, St. Louis, Missouri, USA. Email correspondence with author, January 12, 2016.

7. O'Rourke asks "Are two criteria used when evaluating medical therapy, or are benefit and burden to be combined?" (O'Rourke 2005, 547). Perhaps in low- income settings we have to ask "Are three criteria used when evaluating medical therapy, or are benefit, burden and cost to be combined?"

8. Marcussen notes that the quality of life of a newborn is not easy to assess. He writes "Judgments of well-being in cases of selective nontreatment are often made on the basis of how parents measure what their sense of well-being would be in that circumstance, based on their development and past experiences. The development of the child would be a completely separate and different experience, and the child's experience of overall well-being would likely be different than that of the parents, should their parents ever find themselves in similar circumstances." (Marcussen 2014, 3). This may also be of relevance in regard to the challenge of trying to assess future burdens.

Decision Making in Neonatal End-of-life Scenarios in Low-income Settings

9. The problem of cost is not often considered in many moral or theological reflections, especially when the reflection is done in a first-world setting. In low-income settings, and especially when the state funded healthcare system is inadequate, people do not even go to the hospital in the first place. If they do go, their treatment is usually sub-optimal as they are unable to afford medical items, such as a one-unit blood transfusion, which in the first world can be taken for granted.

10. In the private hospital setting in Manila, ventilation and full support of a sick neonate is $1000 per day. For an insightful video about the effects of poverty on neonatal health care as well as a beautiful testimony of how a Catholic doctor can respond, see the account of Dr Enrique M. Ostrea Jr., M.D., Professor of Pediatrics, Wayne State University, at https://www.youtube.com/watch?v=wcEwdOX3Fl8.

11. There are no unified criteria worldwide for brain death (Wahlster et al. 2015).

12. In low-income settings, families may run out of funds and have to discontinue the life sustaining treatment of their child. Occasional reports exist of attending doctors being hesitant to withdraw the endotracheal (ET) tube as they fear litigation and that they are "committing euthanasia." Instead, they ask the family to withdraw the ET tube. This practice is to be strongly discouraged and doctors should assume responsibility for their patients.

13. Unfortunately, a priest with knowledge of end-of-life moral issues in the pediatric setting is not always available. In some countries, there are Catholic moral bodies that offer a telephone service for ethical consultation. It would be a genuine act of Christian charity if they could also make their services more accessible to those working in low- income settings.

14. O'Rourke notes, "In order to justify forgoing life support, the burden must be judged to be excessive. Determining an excessive burden is often a difficult process. All medical care is a burden in one sense. But an excessive burden makes striving for the continuation of life, or an important good of life, a moral impossibility - or at least very difficult" (O'Rourke 2005, 545-6).

15. Dr. Mackie Quiazon, a former pediatric resident at a government hospital in Manila. Email correspondence with author, March 1, 2016.

References

Allan, Walter C. 2002. The clinical spectrum and prediction of outcome in hypoxic-ischemic encephalopathy. *NeoReviews* 3, n. 6 (June): e108-14.

American Academy of Pediatrics. 2014. Hypothermia and neonatal encephalopathy. *Pediatrics* 133: 1146-50.

Aristotle, *Nicomachean Ethics*. 1953. Trans. By J.A.K. Thomson as The Ethics of Aristotle. London: George Allen & Unwin Ltd.

Camosy, Charles C. 2010. *Too expensive to treat? Finitude, tragedy, and the neonatal ICU.* Grand Rapids: William B. Eerdmans Publishing Company.

Catechism of the Catholic Church. 1997. 2nd ed. Vatican City: Libreria Editrice Vaticana.

Catholic Bishops' Conference of the Philippines. 1997. *Catechism for Filipino Catholics.* Manila, Philippines: ECCCE Word & Life Publications.

Congregation for the Doctrine of the Faith (CDF). 1980. *Declaration on Euthanasia.*

Francis, Pope. 2013. *Evangelii Gaudium.*

Francis, Pope. 2016. *Amoris Laetitia.*

Galvao, Tais F., Marcus T. Silva, Mariana C. Marques, Nelson D. de Oliveira, and Mauricio G. Pereira. 2013. Hypothermia for perinatal brain hypoxia-ischemia in different resource settings: a systematic review. *Journal of Tropical Pediatrics* 59, n. 6: 453-9.

Gloth, F. Michael. 2011. Faith in practice: end-of-life care and the Catholic medical professional. *The Linacre Quarterly* 78, n. 1: 72-81.

John Paul II, Pope. 1987. *Sollicitudo Rei Socialis.*

John Paul II, Pope. 1995. *Evangelium Vitae.*

Liguori, Alphonsus. 1755. *Pratica del confessore.*

Linacre Institute. 2007. Catholic medical decision-making on the concept of futility. *The Linacre Quarterly* 74, n. 3: 258-62.

Marcussen, Michael. 2014. Denying treatment to selected infants. *Ethics and Medics* 39, n. 12: 3-4.

Montaldo, Paolo, Shreela S. Pauliah, Peter J. Lally, Linus Olson, and Sudhin Thayyil. 2015. Cooling in a low-resource environment: Lost in translation. *Seminars in Fetal & Neonatal Medicine* April 20, n. 2: 72-79.

O'Rourke, Kevin D. 2005. The Catholic tradition on forgoing life support. *The National Catholic Bioethics Quarterly* 5, n. 3 (Autumn): 537-53.

Pauliah, Shreela S., Seetha Shankaran, Angie Wade, Ernest B. Cady, and Sudhin Thayyil. 2013. Therapeutic hypothermia for neonatal encephalopathy in low-and middle-income countries: a systematic review and meta-analysis. *PLoS ONE* 8, n. 3: e58834.

Queensland Department of Health, Maternity and Neonatal Clinical Guideline Program. 2016. *Hypoxic-ischaemic encephalopathy.*

Robertson, Charlene M.T. and Max Perlman. 2006. Follow-up of the term infant after hypoxic-ischemic encephalopathy, *Paediatrics and Child Health* 11, n. 5: 278-282.

United States Conference of Catholic Bishops (USCCB). 2009. *Ethical and Religious Directives for Catholic Health Care Services*, 5th ed. Washington, DC: USCCB.

Verhagen, Eduard and Pieter J.J. Sauer. 2005. The Groningen Protocol - euthanasia in severely ill newborns. *New England Journal of Medicine* 352, n. 10: 959-62.

Vizcarrondo, Felipe E. 2014. Neonatal euthanasia: The Groningen Protocol. *The Linacre Quarterly* 81, n. 4: 388-92.

Wahlster, Sarah, Eelco Wijdicks, Pratik Patel, David Greer, J. Claude Hemphill III, Marco Carone, and Farrah Mateen. 2015. Brain death declaration - Practices and perceptions worldwide. *Neurology* 84, n. 18: 1870-79.

Wilkinson, Dominic. 2010. MRI and withdrawal of life support from newborn infants with hypoxic-ischemic encephalopathy. *Pediatrics* 126, n. 2 (August): e451-8.

Wilkinson, Dominic, Lynn Gillam, Jenny Hynson, Jane Sullivan, and Vicky Xafis. n.d. *Caring decisions.* Children's Bioethics Centre, The Royal Children's Hospital, Victoria, Australia.

JUSTICE AND HEALTH CARE: WHEN "ORDINARY" IS EXTRAORDINARY

Summary

In some Asian countries, the poor are often denied access to health care. In the Philippines, we have thousands of Catholic doctors, Catholic nurses, even Catholic administrators, but not a Catholic, understood as "universal," healthcare system available to all. This is a scandal and places heavy emotional and financial burdens on many families who need to pay the healthcare costs of sick loved ones.

The Church teaches the principles of ordinary and extraordinary care, with only the former being morally obligatory. Extraordinary care, that involving excessive burden or cost may be foregone. Many families and healthcare professionals are uncertain about these principles and their application in practice. It would be helpful to more widely disseminate the Catholic Church teaching regarding ordinary and extraordinary care, especially in poor countries, to also avoid unnecessary or futile treatments, especially in critical or end-of-life situations.

In many Asian countries world class medical facilities exist, yet the poor are often denied access to them. In the Philippines, the *Catechism for Filipino Catholics* describes the situation well: "a society where the majority of the population do not enjoy even

Justice And Health Care:
When "ordinary" Is Extraordinary

adequate elementary health care" (Catechism for Filipino Catholics 1997, n. 1039). Yet this health care is a universal right. If we understand "Catholic" as meaning "universal" and "all-embracing," the Philippines cannot be said to have a "Catholic" healthcare system despite having tens of thousands of Catholic doctors, Catholic nurses, even Catholic administrators, as health care is not universally available here and the poor are largely excluded. This is an injustice and a scandal as the Second Vatican Council reminded us (Vatican Council II 1965, n. 88).[1]

The Call of the Church

Ecclesia in Asia notes that "the Church in Asia is committed to becoming still more involved in the care of the sick, since this is a vital part of her mission of offering the saving grace of Christ to the whole person" (John Paul II 1999, n. 36). Many religious men and women, such as the Camillians, dedicate themselves to the care of the sick, but an overall mobilization of the laity is needed.[2] Pope Francis also expressed a concern for the quality of medical care available to the poor and stressed the importance of access to health care: "It is vital that government leaders and financial leaders take heed and broaden their horizons, working to ensure that all citizens have dignified work, education and healthcare" (Francis 2013, n. 205).

Inequity In Healthcare Access

Many state-of-the-art hospitals in Manila offer the latest in world class health care but due to the high cost not all can afford them. In their comprehensive report, titled "The Philippines Health System Review," the Asia Pacific Observatory on Health Systems and Policies confirmed that there exist "considerable inequities in healthcare access and outcomes between socio- economic groups" with a major driver of inequity being "the high cost of accessing and using health care" (APOHSP 2011, xvii). Most Filipinos support the care of their loved ones out of their own pocket. While acknowledging some progress in health reforms, the Observatory concludes that "for many Filipinos, health services have remained less than adequate" (APOHSP 2011, 122) and "reforms in all areas of the Philippine health system are required in order for the country to attain universal health care" (APOHSP 2011, 123).

Corruption as one causative factor

In his visit to the Philippines, Pope Francis made reference to "a society burdened by poverty and corruption" and invited the crowds to "reject every form of corruption which diverts resources from the poor" (Francis 2015). Corruption robs the world's developing countries of more than a trillion dollars every year. If invested in health, this amount could prevent 3.6 million deaths (ONE 2014, 1).[3] Omar Azfar and Tugrul Gurgur report that in the Philippines

> corruption lowers the immunization rate of children, delays the vaccination of newborns, prevents the treatment of patients, discourages the use of public health clinics, reduces

Justice And Health Care:
When "ordinary" Is Extraordinary

satisfaction of households with public health services, and increases waiting time of patients at health clinics. (Azfar and Gurgur 2008, 197)

How many deaths might be prevented in the Philippines if embezzled money had instead been invested in creating a universally accessible healthcare system?[4] It means people like Juan (name changed to protect anonymity) are denied the possibility of reasonable health care. Juan is a 24-year-old man who works with poultry. He presented to the emergency room with fever and strong headaches. He was diagnosed with cerebral cryptococcal infection. The medicine prescribed, a powerful anti-fungal, costs $100 per day. How long can he afford that treatment with a salary of $7 per day?

Exorbitant cost of medicines

Drug prices in the Philippines are recognized to be among the highest in Asia. Dr. Dennis B. Batangan reports that "pharmaceuticals are expensive in the Philippines in comparison to prices in neighboring countries such as Thailand, Malaysia and Indonesia" (Batangan et al. 2006, 7). Less than 30 percent of the population has access to essential medicines. In a telling article Annie Ruth Sabangan reports that

> sixteen of the top 20 drug companies in the Philippines are multinational firms with combined sales of P58.23 billion in 2007, nearly eight times more than the Philippines' P7.39 billion GDP in 2008 ... Their sales represent about 82% of the total volume sales

of foreign pharmaceutical firms in the country. (Sabangan 2009)

Pharmaceutical sales are big business, and to be convinced of this one need only walk the corridors of any large hospital here to purvey the incessant hordes of drug reps plying their wares. Doctors should thus strive to maintain a good ethical code of conduct lest the lure of perks from the pharmaceutical industry unduly influence their prescribing habits.

WHEN ORDINARY BECOMES EXTRAORDINARY

A bout of prolonged sickness, an accident, or an end-of-life situation can tip patients and their families into financial despair. For a poor family a relatively straightforward treatment such as a blood transfusion may simply be beyond their budget. In a developed context, it would be generally inconceivable to consider a blood transfusion as "extraordinary" treatment from a financial point of view. However, in the Philippines when patients need a transfusion, they have to pay from $10 up to $225 per unit of blood depending on the type of hospital they are staying in (charity or private). This can be exorbitantly expensive in a country where the minimum daily wage is $10. What is ordinary care in developed countries often becomes extraordinary in the developing world.

What to do when a loved one is critically ill

When loved ones reach the end of their earthly life, it can be a psychologically and emotionally draining experience for them and for their family. Sometimes

Justice And Health Care:
When "ordinary" Is Extraordinary

the family can feel caught in a quandary - the desire for their loved ones to live on and survive but also the desire that they do not suffer too much unnecessarily. In the Filipino setting, the final sickness of a loved one not only places heavy affective burdens on the family but also financial ones. Obviously loving concern should be shown by trying to ensure good treatment of sick loved ones, but there may be some situations where it can be very hard for the family or even impossible to provide the necessary care. They may want to continue care, but simply run out of money. And even with sufficient funds, situations arrive when nothing more should be done, only to accept that the time has come for the suffering of the patient to come to its natural end.

Avoid euthanasia

Believing that God is the giver of life, we have no right to take it away prematurely. Euthanasia needs to be avoided. It is defined in the Church's *Declaration on Euthanasia* as "an action or an omission which of itself or by intention causes death, in order that all suffering may in this way be eliminated" (Sacred Congregation for the Doctrine of the Faith 1980, part II). The *Catechism of the Catholic Church* states,

> direct euthanasia consists in putting an end to the lives of handicapped, sick, or dying persons. Thus an act or omission which, of itself or by intention, causes death in order to eliminate suffering constitutes a murder gravely contrary to the dignity of the human person and the

respect due to the living God, his Creator. The error of judgment into which one can fall in good faith does not change the nature of this murderous act, which must always be forbidden and excluded. (Catechism 1997, n. 2277)

Euthanasia can thus be performed by *act* or *omission*. An "act" could include giving a lethal injection to a patient, and an "omission" would involve failing to provide life-saving medical care with the intention and result of causing the patient's death.

Discontinuing burdensome or futile treatment

In most cases in the Philippines, the problem will not be a desire to commit euthanasia. Rather, problems come in knowing when "enough is enough", or when to say "no" to further unnecessary treatment. We would not want our loved ones to undergo unnecessary or futile ("useless") treatments and to make them suffer a treatment that would not be helpful. The *Catechism of the Catholic Church* has some very helpful advice: "Discontinuing medical procedures that are burdensome, dangerous, extraordinary, or disproportionate to the expected outcome can be legitimate; it is the refusal of 'over-zealous' treatment. Here one does not will to cause death; one's inability to impede it is merely accepted" (Catechism 1997, n. 2278).

Discontinuing the treatment such as turning off a ventilator when it has become excessively burdensome is *not* euthanasia. It is rather the acceptance that medically nothing more can be done. There is no

Justice And Health Care: When "ordinary" Is Extraordinary

desire to kill the patient, rather there is an acceptance of our human, medical, and even financial limits in front of sickness and death.

Family tensions

At times, the final sickness of a loved one can cause various family tensions to surface. A real-life scenario (based on a similar case) illustrates this: a grandmother, 85 years old, with heart failure and respiratory failure, has a family who loves her very much and wants to do everything possible to "save" her. One daughter, who has lived with her and cared for her for many years, peacefully accepts that the end is near. But a son who has spent years away in the US wants his mother to live so that he can spend time with her. In these situations, there can be conflicting views in the family. Dialogue is important to clarify the position of each one. It is important to be aware that sometimes the sick one becomes like a pawn in a game of chess, and often unreconciled family issues can arise in these stressful and tense moments.

Let the patient decide!

The desire and request of the patient should be taken into consideration - the patient is the first one to decide the steps of their treatment. The *Catechism* teaches that decisions "should be made by the patient if he is competent and able or, if not, by those legally titled to act for the patient, whose reasonable will and legitimate interests must always be respected" (Catechism 1997, n. 2278).

We should take care to avoid deciding everything for the patient. Family members sometimes make the excuse that their loved one could not bear to hear the news especially if negative, but perhaps the one who cannot bear it is them and they are just projecting their fears. It is a grave injustice when all the family and friends know, even the neighbors, but often the patient is left in the dark.

What care would be necessary?

A caring doctor can give very helpful advice about the treatment required. At times the family may feel pressure to do everything possible to keep their loved ones alive but our heart needs to be guided also by our head. It helps to try to be objective in these situations, not to be taken solely by sad or heavy feelings. A family may feel guilty when nothing more can be done and inadvertently put their sick loved one through further unnecessary suffering which will not help the patient. The patient, doctor, and family may all decide beforehand not to undertake resuscitation, deeming it over-aggressive or futile, in line with Church teaching.

The family should avoid the temptation to subsequently change that decision in moments of medical crisis except for valid, serious, and medically justifiable reasons, not merely misplaced emotional ones. Overly aggressive and futile treatment should never be employed just to try to meet unrealistic demands.

Justice And Health Care:
When "ordinary" Is Extraordinary

"ORDINARY MEANS" ARE OBLIGATORY

One very helpful principle here from Catholic healthcare ethics is the principle of ordinary means. Stated by Gerard Kelly, the principle of ordinary means reads, "Ordinary means are all medicines, treatments and operations which offer a reasonable hope of benefit and which can be obtained and used without excessive expense, pain or other inconvenience" (Kelly 1951, 551).

Ordinary means are morally obligatory. So, if the treatment does not offer reasonable hope, is excessively expensive, or is inconvenient, then it would be classified as an extraordinary intervention and would only be optional and not be morally obligatory - a conclusion which can give peace of mind to the family who may be facing a dilemma as to what is the correct course of action to take.

What if no funds are available?

As health care here is not free, many families find that the final sickness of a loved one puts them under tremendous financial burdens especially if the illness is prolonged or complicated. A family should do all they reasonably can to care for their loved one, but there may come a moment when the treatment proposed, such as a ventilator, is simply too costly, or if the treatment is prolonged, such as dialysis, funds run out. They may even decide to remove their sick loved one from the hospital and to spend their remaining time together at home. The Church clearly teaches that all things practically possible should be done, such as basic care of the person and providing appropriate nutrition and hydration. However, there will be times when the family simply cannot afford further care and it would be considered as extraordinary treatment.

Extraordinary means of preserving life are those treatments, medicines, and operations which are gravely burdensome to the patient, and which cannot be obtained or used without excessive expense, pain, or other inconvenience or which, if used, would not offer a reasonable hope of benefit to the patient. Extraordinary treatments such as excessively expensive treatments or operations way beyond the reasonable effort or budget of the family are optional and not morally obligatory. The Catholic Medical Association (United States), in their guidelines note that

> While people may use extraordinary means, they are not morally obligated to do so since earthy life for humans is not an absolute good and because, at some point, medical interventions are no longer effective and/or because the costs and burdens of medical interventions are out of proportion to the good of earthly life that they are intended to serve. (Catholic Medical Association 2007, 2A)

This frees the family from feeling over-guilty when situations come when they run out of funds. And even if funds are available, not everything that is technically or medically possible would necessarily be ethical. Sometimes we just need to accept the will of God.

Justice And Health Care:
When "ordinary" Is Extraordinary

ORDINARY OR EXTRAORDINARY?

How can we know when a treatment is ordinary (thus morally obligatory) or extraordinary (only optional)? The Church gives us helpful advice: "by studying the type of treatment to be used, its degree of complexity or risk, its cost and the possibilities of using it, and comparing these elements with the result that can be expected, taking into account the state of the sick person and his or her physical and moral resources" (Sacred Congregation for the Doctrine of the Faith 1980, part IV).[5]

In determining whether a treatment is ordinary or extraordinary one should not merely consider the degree of technology involved. It would be erroneous to state that "the treatment is ordinary, but the family could not afford it." If the family cannot afford it, then the treatment is not ordinary but extraordinary. Ordinary (or extraordinary) is not simply a technical explanation of the complexity of a treatment, but rather a description of the overall set of circumstances including the treatment proposed, the burden imposed, the degree of success, pain incurred, as well as the financial situation of the patient and family. For patient A, kidney dialysis can be "extra- ordinary" because it is not available in his geographical location and to receive it three times per week would result in an insurmountable travel burden. For patient B, the same dialysis may be available locally but be "extraordinary" because the cost may be beyond the available resources of the family. For patient C, dialysis may be accessible and affordable, but having a minimal chance of success it can be deemed "extraordinary."

In some ways a dynamic and real-time analysis of the patient and his or her medical situation needs to be performed. On day one of a sickness, a family could have funds to pay for a ventilator (so it could be "ordinary"); but on day 10 their funds may be exhausted and thus the same treatment (a ventilator) can become extraordinary. Or a patient receiving chemotherapy may tolerate the first round of drugs and expect a reasonable chance of success. But if the cancer proves resistant, further rounds of chemotherapy, which are much less likely to cure and more likely to become increasingly burdensome for the patient, would be "extraordinary" and thus not obligatory. Further examples could be given but the point has been made the situation of a sick person needs to be continually re-assessed, and what is judged "ordinary" treatment may later become "extraordinary."

Hospital bias may exist

It may be that, in healthcare systems that are subsidized by the state, pressure may be put on families to coerce or "encourage" them not to pursue certain treatment options. Stopping such treatments could thus save the state large sums of money. In other countries, such as the Philippines, where adequate, state-funded coverage is lacking, patients and families have to pay for the medical services. Here the opposite scenario may be encountered - the hospital or attending doctors

Justice And Health Care:
When "ordinary" Is Extraordinary

may over-encourage a patient or family to pursue a treatment option that is not so viable. This is a very sorry state of affairs especially in a Catholic country like the Philippines where the hospital and attending physicians may be motivated by financial gain rather than merely patient welfare.

Can treatment plans be specified in advance?

Various options exist for trying to decide in advance what treatment courses to take or avoid. Examples include so-called living wills, advanced directives, power of attorney, and POLST (physician orders for life-sustaining treatment).[6] One challenge is it is difficult to foresee all the possible future health scenarios. Perhaps this can be illustrated through a humorous example recounted by a professor of bioethics at the Regina Apostolorum University in Rome to show that what we specify regarding future medical interventions may be subject to misinterpretation. A man is taking sips of his beer every few seconds and playing with his iPad and iPod. He turned on the TV, and there was a program on euthanasia. On screen a man was hooked up to a life support machine and receiving fluids through a drip. He called his wife and said "Darling, if you ever see me dependent on liquids and relying on technology just shoot me!" This could be understood to be an instruction for the here and now as indeed this man was dependent on his beer (liquids) and his iPod and iPad (technology).

Translating this anecdote into a real-life medical scenario of a chronic debilitating illness, I may state today that I do not wish to be put on a ventilator, but what if, after writing and signing such a statement, the next day I fall and sustain a head injury that requires a ventilator for 1 or 2 days until my brain swelling subsides? It is different to be on a ventilator for 2 days or 2 months.

ACCEPTING GOD'S WILL

When the family is desperate, they can even search for alternative cures and ignore the advice of the doctors. In Tobit 2:10 we hear the complaint "I went to see some doctors for a cure, but the more they anointed my eyes with various ointments, the worse I became." And in Luke's gospel we are told of "a woman afflicted with hemorrhages for twelve years, who had spent her whole livelihood on doctors and was unable to be cured by anyone" (Lk 8:43). It is also true that we should "Hold the physician in honor, for he is essential to you, and God it was who established his profession. From God the doctor has his wisdom ... He who is a sinner toward his Maker will be defiant toward the doctor" (Sir 38:15). Sometimes in desperation a family may be willing to try anything, but care should be taken as sometimes sadness or fear of impending death of a loved one can impede good judgment. Instead of seeking a weird and wonderful cure there are times when one has to accept that the time has come for our loved one to depart from this earthly life.

Even if we pray for a miracle God does most of his good work through everyday ways. The real miracle will not be that we do not die, but rather that he gives

Justice And Health Care:
When "ordinary" Is Extraordinary

us the gift of eternal life. We hope to be with our loved ones forever, but not in this life. This is the promise of our Lord and the hope of our faith. "He will wipe every tear from their eyes, and there shall be no more death or mourning, wailing or pain, for the old order has passed away" (Rev 21:4).

May we place all our trust and hope in our Lord, the giver of Life, who announces, "I am the Resurrection and the Life; whoever believes in me, even if he dies, will live" (John 11:25). Jesus, our Good Doctor, pray for us!

CONCLUSION

All Catholics should be concerned about universal health care for all. As William May reminded us,

> we the people have a strict obligation in justice to see to it that the health care needs of the poor in our society are met. In addition, since we are obligated to honor the universal common good, we need to think of the health care needs of the millions of poor throughout the world. Although we are not obligated to do the impossible, and although we simply cannot do everything, we must seek to do something to bring to people in other societies a decent minimum in health care. (May 1989)

A simple step could be to remind doctors who may be working far from their native lands not only to enjoy the perks and salary of their new homeland but also to consider the medical ill fortune of many compatriots back home. I call on all Filipino doctors, especially the many working in the United States, in some of the world's most advanced hospitals and institutions, to please resist the temptations of careerism and materialism and instead to spare a thought, a prayer, and perhaps even a dollar for millions of their brothers and sisters who lack access to even basic health care. The call of Christ, "I was sick and you healed me" (Matt 25:36), can remind them of the duty of their mission - not only to become materially well off, but to be rich in mercy and compassion.

Notes

1. "Do not let men, then, be scandalized because some countries with a majority of citizens who are counted as Christians have an abundance of wealth, whereas others are deprived of the necessities of life and are tormented with hunger, disease, and every kind of misery" (Vatican Council II 1965, n. 88).

2. In Asia, the lay have been referred to as the "sleeping giant" (Cervellera 2010).

3. "ONE estimates that as many as 3.6 million deaths could be prevented each year in the world's developing countries if action is taken to end the secrecy that allows corruption and criminality to thrive and the recovered revenues were invested in health system" (ONE 2014).

4. For more information on how corruption affects delivery of healthcare services see Vian (2008). Also, Olarte and Chua (2005).

5. These norms are repeated in USCCB (2009), dirs. 56 and 57.

6. Some Catholic experts have cautioned against the use of POLST, and suggest the use of a modified format (see Brugger et al. 2013).

References

Asia Pacific Observatory on Health Systems and Policies (APOHSP). 2011. The Philippines health system review. *Health Systems in Transition* 1(2).

Azfar, Omar and Tugrul Gurgur. 2008. Does corruption affect health outcomes in the Philippines? *Economics of Governance* 9(3): 197-244.

Batangan, Dennis, Chona Echavez, Anthony Aldrin Santiago, Amparo de la Cruz, and Engracia Santos. 2006. The prices people have to pay for medicines in the Philippines. Institute of Philippine Culture, Ateneo de Manila University, Philippines, in collaboration with Health Action International/World Health Organization Department of Health, Philippines.

Brugger, Christian, Louis Breschi, Edith Mary Hart, Mark Kummer, John Lane, Peter Morrow, Franklin Smith, William Toffler, Marissa Beffel, John Brehany, Sara Buscher, and Rita Marker. 2013. The POLST paradigm and form: Facts and analysis. *Linacre Quarterly* 80(2): 103-138.

Catholic Bishops' Conference of the Philippines, 1997. *Catechism for Filipino Catholics.* Manila, Philippines: ECCCE Word & Life Publications.

Catholic Medical Association. 2007. Guidelines on resolving conflicts about treatments deemed "futile."

Catechism of the Catholic Church. 1997. 2nd ed. Vatican City: Libreria Editrice Vaticana.

Cervellera, Bernardo. 2010. Lay Catholics in Asia: A "sleeping giant" that is waking up. AsiaNews.it. September 2.

Francis, Pope. 2013. *Evangelii Gaudium.*

Francis, Pope. 2015. Pope's homily at mass with Filipino bishops, priests, religious. January 16.

John Paul II, Pope. 1999. *Ecclesia in Asia.*

Kelly, Gerard K. 1951. The duty to preserve life. *Theological Studies* 12(4): 551.

May, William. 1989. Health care and the poor. Ethics & Medics 14(12) (December).

Olarte, Avigail M., and Yvonne T. Chua. 2005. Up to 70% of local healthcare funds lost to corruption. Philippine Center for Investigative Journalism, May 2.

ONE. 2014. The trillion-dollar scandal.

Sabangan, Annie Ruth. 2009. For profitable RP drug industry, price cut is a pill that's hard to swallow. GMA News Online. September 15.

Sacred Congregation for the Doctrine of the Faith. 1980. *Declaration on Euthanasia*,

United States Conference of Catholic Bishops (USCCB). 2009. *Ethical and religious directives for Catholic health care services*, 5th ed. Washington, DC: USCCB.

Vatican Council II. 1965. *Gaudium et Spes.*

Vian, Taryn. 2008. Review of corruption in the health sector: Theory, methods and interventions. *Health Policy and Planning* 23: 83-94.

THE LION ROARS
- OPPOSING EUTHANASIA AND ASSISTED SUICIDE IN THE SPIRIT OF CARDINAL VON GALEN

Summary

Part 1 of this essay begins with a snapshot of the life and preaching of Cardinal Clemens August von Galen, a man of courage who actively resisted the programmatic termination of the elderly, infirm, and disabled - the so-called "unproductive" - by the Nazis in Germany during World War 2.

Time has moved on, yet in Part 2 we will be disturbed to see, once again, the growing trend of eliminating "unworthy" lives through euthanasia and assisted suicide in our modern, throwaway culture. An overview of Church teaching in these areas will be given, including the new Vatican charter on healthcare, and "Samaritanus Bonus" (Good Samaritan), a 2020 document from the Congregation for the Doctrine of the Faith (CDF, now called the Dicastery for the Doctrine of the Faith, DDF) "on the care of persons in the critical and terminal phases of life."

Part 1: The Lion Who Roared

Von Galen was known as the "Lion of Münster." Standing over six feet and six inches tall (around 2 meters), he was a German bishop - and later elected Cardinal - who roared against the Nazis during

The Lion Roars - Opposing Euthanasia

World War 2, particularly in his opposition to their euthanasia program.

In his homilies and pastoral letters, von Galen criticized the Gestapo for their abuses against human rights. His motto was "Nec laudibus, nec timore" (commonly paraphrased: Neither praise nor threats will distance me from God) and he lived it to the full. He was unfazed upon receiving intimidating letters from Hermann Göring, the Reich Marshall of the Greater German Reich. Göring accused von Galen of sabotaging "the strength of resistance of the German people in the midst of a war" (Utrecht 2016, 258). to which von Galen replied that he felt himself obliged to do so because of the actions of certain circles that, behind the back of the German troops, carry on a battle against the Christian religion and the Catholic Church and against reverence for the inalienable fundamental rights of the human person, and endanger the inner unity and power of resistance of the German people. (Utrecht 2016, 259)

Other opponents of von Galen included the notorious Joseph Goebbels, the Minister of Propaganda for the Nazis, who was hesitant to attack von Galen (other Nazis had suggested that von Galen should be hanged) as he feared the backlash from the bishop's supporters in his diocese, although he did state that "revenge should be enjoyed, not hot, but cold." In a conversation over dinner in July 1942, even Hitler told his companions that after Germany wins the war, he would reckon with von Galen "down to the last penny." (Utrecht 2016, 260)

JESUS THE DIVINE PHYSICIAN

The "Unproductive"

The Lion of Münster really roared upon hearing of the introduction of a euthanasia program organized by the Nazis. He preached three famous sermons in 1941 where he condemned the atrocities of the Third Reich, particularly their introduction of a program for killing those deemed mentally ill and "unproductive." The excerpts below are from von Galen's sermon on Sunday, August 3, 1941, in St. Lambert's Church, Münster, Germany. The Sunday Gospel was taken from chapter 19 of St. Luke, where Jesus, surveying the happenings, weeps (Lk. 19:42ff).[1]

> These numerous unexpected deaths of the mentally ill are not the result of natural causes, but are deliberately brought about; that in these cases that doctrine is being followed, that one can put an end to so-called "worthless life," that is, can kill innocent persons, if one believes that their life is of no more value to the people and the state; a horrible doctrine, that would justify the murder of the innocent, that gives a fundamental license for the violent killing of those invalids, cripples, incurable sick, and weak old persons who are no longer able to work! (Utrecht 2016, 238)

The bishop, ever attentive to the "signs of the times," gave concrete details of the events that were taking place (see Matthew 16:3).

> Already on the 26th of July I had made a most earnest appeal to the Provincial Administration

of the Province of Westphalia, which is responsible for these institutions, to which the sick are sent for care and healing. It was no use! The first transport of innocent victims condemned to death has gone from Marienthal! And I have heard that 800 patients have been transported from the Institute for Care and Healing of Warstein.

So we must assume that these poor, defenseless sick people will sooner or later be killed. Why? Not because they have committed a capital crime; not because they have attacked their caregivers in such wise that these were left with no recourse to save their own lives in self-defence other than the use of violence against their attackers. These would be cases in which, in addition to the killing of armed enemies in a just war, use of force even to the extent of killing is allowed and, not rarely, required. No, not for such reasons do these unfortunate sick people have to die, but rather because, according to the judgment of some official, according to the opinion of some commission, they have become "unworthy of life"; because according to this opinion they belong to the category of "unproductive" fellow countrymen. It is judged that they can no longer produce goods; they are like an old machine that does not work anymore; they are like an old horse that has become incurably lame; they are like a cow that no longer gives milk. What

> does one do with such old machines? They are scrapped. What does one do with a lame horse or an unproductive cow?
>
> No. I will not continue this comparison to the end, so frightful is its appropriateness and its illuminating power!
>
> We are not dealing with machines, or horses or cows, which are created in order to serve [human persons], to produce goods for [them]! One may destroy or kill such beings when they no longer fulfill this purpose. No, here we are dealing with people, our fellow human beings, our brothers and sisters! Poor people, sick people, unproductive people, granted! But does that mean they have lost the right to life? Do you, do I, have the right to life only so long as we are productive, only so long as others acknowledge that we are productive? (Utrecht 2016, 240-241)

Speaking from the heart, with such frankness and courage, his preaching had a powerful impact. He continued:

> If that principle is accepted and made use of, that one can kill "unproductive" people, then woe to us all, when we become old and weak! If one can kill unproductive people, then woe to the disabled who have sacrificed their health or their limbs in the process of production! If unproductive people can be disposed of by violent means, then woe to our brave soldiers

> who return to their homeland severely wounded, as cripples, as invalids! Once it is granted that people have the right to kill "unproductive" fellow human beings - even if at the moment it affects only the poor defenseless mentally ill - then in principle the right has been given to murder all unproductive people: the incurably ill, the cripples who are unable to work, those who have become incapacitated because of work or war; then the right has been given to murder all of us, once we become weak with age and therefore unproductive. (Utrecht 2016, 241-242).

The appalling image of wounded soldiers having survived battle and returning from conflict and yet potentially being put to death in their own land through euthanasia sent shockwaves through the German people and infuriated the Nazis. Von Galen continued his homily:

> All that will be required is for some secret order to come down, that the process which has been tested on the mentally ill should now be extended to other "unproductive" people, to those with incurable lung disease, to the infirm elderly, to the severely wounded soldiers. Then the life of none of us is safe. Some commission can put [anyone] on the list of the "unproductive" who are, according to its judgment, "unworthy of life." And no policemen will protect [them], and no court will take notice of [their] murder and subject

> the murderers to the prescribed punishment! (Utrecht 2016, 242).

Copies of the homilies were made and distributed far and wide. Even the Allied powers were said to have used these as propaganda against the Germans! Von Galen also asks a very pointed question, one that makes us shirk in horror when we consider the travesty against life committed by many healthcare professionals and Christians today in their support for and lack of defiance against assisted suicide and euthanasia.

> Who will then be able to trust [their] doctor? Perhaps [the doctor] will report the patient as "unproductive" and receive the order to kill [them]. It is unthinkable what degeneration of morals, what universal mistrust will find its way even into the family, if this frightening doctrine is tolerated, taken up, and followed. Woe to humanity, woe to our German people, if the holy commandment of God, "Thou shalt not kill," which the Lord gave on Sinai amid thunder and lightning, which God the Creator wrote into the conscience of [humankind] from the beginning, is not only broken, but if this breach is tolerated and taken up as a regular practice without punishment! (Utrecht 2016, 242).

Part 2: The Situation We Now Face

Von Galen's homilies have much relevance for the situation today where various persons in society and the medical profession itself are campaigning for programs of euthanasia and assisted suicide. Von Galen mentioned that those targeted were the "unproductive"; this is echoed today, where "the current socio-cultural context is gradually eroding the awareness of what makes human life precious. In fact, it is increasingly valued on the basis of its efficiency and utility, to the point of considering as "discarded lives" or "unworthy lives" those who do not meet this criterion." (Francis 2020, n. 7)

Pope Francis frequently laments the throwaway culture that we are living in as "human beings are themselves considered consumer goods to be used and then discarded. We have created a 'throw away' culture which is now spreading." (Francis 2013, n. 53) Lives deemed not worthy of living are increasingly being ended through euthanasia and assisted suicide.[2]

Euthanasia is currently legal in an ever-growing list of countries, including The Netherlands, Belgium, Luxembourg, Canada, Colombia, Spain, and New Zealand. Assisted suicide is also permitted in Canada (Medical Assistance in Dying - MAiD), the United States (in California, Colorado, the District of Columbia, Hawaii, Maine, New Jersey, New Mexico, Oregon, Vermont, and Washington), and Australia (Voluntary Assisted Dying [VAD] is allowed in Victoria, Western Australia, and, most recently, in Tasmania).

We can be sure that none of this legislation would have succeeded without some support from the healthcare sector. Such "legitimation of assisted suicide and euthanasia is a sign of the degradation of legal systems." (Congregation for the Doctrine of the Faith 2020, V.1)

Quality of life

Discussions surrounding euthanasia or assisted suicide are founded at times on the premise of "quality of life."[3] (Congregation for the Doctrine of the Faith 2020, IV). The Congregation for the Doctrine of the Faith produced a helpful document called *Samaritanus Bonus*, which in part IV gives a helpful explanation of some aspects surrounding "quality of life" judgments:

> Among the obstacles that diminish our sense of the profound intrinsic value of every human life, the first lies in the notion of "dignified death" as measured by the standard of the "quality of life," which a utilitarian anthropological perspective sees in terms "primarily related to economic means, to 'well-being,' to the beauty and enjoyment of physical life, forgetting the other, more profound, interpersonal, spiritual and religious dimensions of existence". In this perspective, life is viewed as worthwhile only if it has, in the judgment of the individual or of third parties, an acceptable degree of quality as measured by the possession or lack of particular psychological or physical functions, or sometimes simply by the presence

of psychological discomfort. According to this view, a life whose quality seems poor does not deserve to continue. Human life is thus no longer recognized as a value in itself. (Congregation for the Doctrine of the Faith 2020, IV)

In a recent article titled "The 'Quality of Life' Error," Fr. T. Pacholczyk, director of education at the National Catholic Bioethics Center, writes:

> The clearest rebuttal of the "Quality of Life" error I've come across was from a 64-year-old retired Boeing computer programmer named John Peyton (1945-2009). He lived in Kent, Washington, and had an unusually aggressive form of amyotrophic lateral sclerosis, or ALS, commonly known as Lou Gehrig's disease. The disease made him totally dependent on Patricia, his wife of 40 years. She dressed him, fed him, and regularly shifted his body position in the living room recliner where he spent his declining months.
>
> When he was interviewed by Laura Ingraham of Fox News, he said, "I'm one of those people who is somewhat of a target of the initiative and I don't know how we as a society could really consider making doctors into killers."
>
> Laura countered: "John, I think a lot of people who are for this type of assisted suicide would say, 'Look, what about the quality of life?' 'Look, you know, people suffering like you -

what kind of quality of life do you really have?' What do you say to those people?"

His reply was as brilliant as it was simple:

> I have a marvelous quality of life! Right now I am totally dependent. I can do nothing for myself. I'm effectively paralyzed. But I have a family. I have friends. I have my church community. I have loving support all around me. I don't understand how anyone could deny that I have a very high quality of life, and it gets me to understand and be compassionate toward those without the support that I have. Rather than giving them the temptation to kill themselves, we should be trying to figure out how to help them to have the quality of life I enjoy. (Pacholczyk 2021, 1-2)

A Not so Pain-free Death

Bernadette Flood, a pharmacist in Dublin, wrote a fascinating, if slightly gruesome, letter to the British Medical Journal in response to the news that Spain would become the sixth country worldwide to allow euthanasia and assisted suicide. (Rada 2021, 147) Her letter begins thus:

> Dear Editor, many healthcare professionals, politicians and members of the general public who support the introduction of assisted suicide and/or euthanasia may be under the impression that the method of dying they support would

> be achieved by the administration of "a pill". This is not the case. (Flood 2021, 2498)

She then cites some problematic issues related to assisted suicide and/or euthanasia:

- The dying process can take up to 30 hours or more.
- Reports exist of people re-emerging from a coma and sitting up during the dying process.
- Family members have reported having to scrape powder from 100 plus capsules with toothpicks to produce bitter powder to be mixed with sugar syrup.
- A number of medicines used in assisted suicide and/or euthanasia were previously used in executions.

For many supporters of such a death by medication, her conclusion is eye-opening: "The process of assisted suicide and/or euthanasia cannot guarantee a peaceful, pain free, dignified death."

Church Teaching

Here we will take a brief overview of some pertinent points from relevant Church teaching.

> With her mission to transmit to the faithful the grace of the Redeemer and the holy law of God already discernible in the precepts of the natural moral law, the Church is obliged to intervene in order to exclude once again all ambiguity in the

teaching of the Magisterium concerning euthanasia and assisted suicide, even where these practices have been legalized. (Congregation for the Doctrine of the Faith 2020, V)

The Second Vatican Council taught that euthanasia and willful self-destruction (such as occurs through assisted suicide) "poison human society" and are, moreover, "a supreme dishonor to the Creator." (Paul VI 1965, n. 27). In the *Catechism of the Catholic Church*, we find the following teaching:

> Those whose lives are diminished or weakened deserve special respect. Sick or handicapped persons should be helped to lead lives as normal as possible. (Catechism of the Catholic Church 1997, n. 2276)

> Whatever its motives and means, direct euthanasia consists in putting an end to the lives of handicapped, sick, or dying persons. It is morally unacceptable. Thus, an act or omission which, of itself or by intention, causes death in order to eliminate suffering constitutes a murder gravely contrary to the dignity of the human person and to the respect due to the living God, [their] Creator. The error of judgment into which one can fall in good faith does not change the nature of this murderous act, which must always be forbidden and excluded. (Catechism of the Catholic Church 1997, n. 2277)

The Lion Roars - Opposing Euthanasia

The 1980 *Declaration on Euthanasia* from the Sacred Congregation for the Doctrine of the Faith states:

> By euthanasia is understood an action or an omission which of itself or by intention causes death, in order that all suffering may in this way be eliminated. Euthanasia's terms of reference, therefore, are to be found in the intention of the will and in the methods used. It is necessary to state firmly once more that nothing and no one can in any way permit the killing of an innocent human being, whether a fetus or an embryo, an infant or an adult, an old person, or one suffering from an incurable disease, or a person who is dying. (Congregation for the Doctrine of the Faith 1980, II)

When a sick and suffering person seems to be requesting assisted suicide, beneath this plea there is an underlying garbled cry for help, for love, and for life. The *Declaration* incisively teaches:

> The pleas of gravely ill people who sometimes ask for death are not to be understood as implying a true desire for euthanasia; in fact, it is almost always a case of an anguished plea for help and love. What a sick person needs, besides medical care, is love, the human and super-natural warmth with which the sick person can and ought to be surrounded by all those close to him or her, parents and children, doctors and nurses. (Congregation for the Doctrine of the Faith 1980, II)

The same Declaration explains that even though a person may not be fully aware of their erroneous choice of euthanasia, it is still an objective wrong.

> It may happen that, by reason of prolonged and barely tolerable pain, for deeply personal or other reasons, people may be led to believe that they can legitimately ask for death or obtain it for others. Although in these cases the guilt of the individual may be reduced or completely absent, nevertheless the error of judgment into which the conscience falls, perhaps in good faith, does not change the nature of this act of killing, which will always be in itself something to be rejected. (Congregation for the Doctrine of the Faith 1980, II)

The 2017 Vatican charter for healthcare workers strongly denounces euthanasia as a defeat, a crime, a backward step, and a homicidal act which no end can justify. (Pontifical Council for Pastoral Assistance to Health Care Workers 2017) It teaches further that "one's attitude toward the sick person in the terminal stage of [their] illness is a test of the professionalism and ethical responsibilities of health care workers." (Pontifical Council for Pastoral Assistance to Health Care Workers 2017, n. 145) The new charter also stresses the importance of good palliative care:

> A sick person in the terminal stage of [their] illness should receive all forms of care that allow for alleviation of the painfulness of the dying

process. These correspond to so-called palliative care which [,] together with care for [their] physical, psychological, and spiritual needs, tends to create a loving presence around the dying person and [their] family members. (Pontifical Council for Pastoral Assistance to Health Care Workers 2017, n. 147)

The charter also underlines that euthanasia and assisted suicide are always a wrong choice.

> [Medical] personnel and other health care workers - faithful to their task of "always being at the service of life and assisting it to the end" - cannot lend themselves to any act of euthanasia, not even at the request of the interested party, much less of [their] relatives. Indeed, there is no right to dispose arbitrarily of one's own life, and for this reason no health care worker can become the executor of a nonexistent right. (Pontifical Council for Pastoral Assistance to Health Care Workers 2017, n. 169)

For this reason, "euthanasia and assisted suicide are a defeat for those who theorize about them, who decide upon them, or who practice them." (Pontifical Council for Pastoral Assistance to Health Care Workers 2017, n. 170)

Next we will summarize some interesting points from *Samaritanus Bonus* (Good Samaritan), the document on the care of persons in the critical and terminal phases of life. The introduction to the letter points out that "every technical advance in healthcare calls for growth in moral discernment to avoid an unbalanced and dehumanizing use of the technologies especially in the critical or terminal stages of human life." (Congregation for the Doctrine of the Faith 2020, Introduction)[3]

Discussing care for one's neighbor in the spirit of the good Samaritan who takes responsibility for the wounded patient, the document states that

> every individual who cares for the sick (physician, nurse, relative, volunteer, pastor) has the moral responsibility to apprehend the fundamental and inalienable good that is the human person. They should adhere to the highest standards of self-respect and respect for others by embracing, safeguarding and promoting human life until natural death. (Congregation for the Doctrine of the Faith 2020, I)

The document points out that the cross of Christ provides a point of reference for the sick person. Many were at the cross - functionaries of the Roman state, soldiers, mockers, those distracted/indifferent/resentful. They are at the cross but do not "remain" with the suffering one. "In intensive care units or centers for chronic illness care, one can be present merely as a functionary, or as someone who 'remains' with the sick." (Congregation for the Doctrine of the Faith 2020, II) This is an important part of Christian witness - not to abandon the sick at their most vulnerable but to be with them.

> Those who assist persons with chronic illnesses or in the terminal stages of life must be able to "know how to stay", to keep vigil, with those who suffer the anguish of death, "to console" them, to be with them in their loneliness, to be an abiding with that can instill hope. By means of the faith and charity expressed in the intimacy of the soul, the caregiver can experience the pain of another, can be open to a personal relationship with the weak that expands the horizons of life beyond death, and thus can become a presence full of hope. (Congregation for the Doctrine of the Faith 2020, V)

Working hard for the grim reaper

Many groups are working hard for the grim reaper. Compassion & Choices, a U.S.-based dignity-in-dying group, proudly boasts of its achievements in campaigning hard in its mission to legalize assisted suicide: "We [have] organized hearings ... and inspired strong and robust grassroots efforts. Volunteer advocates shared their stories and support through emails, phone calls, lobby days, social media and videos." (Anonymous, 2021, 4)

In front of such convinced, if slightly deranged, campaigns, the Christian response is often one of apathy, indifference, commodity, silence, or mediocrity. Von Galen, recalling a statement in a homily by Cardinal Pacelli (who later became Pope Pius XII), said, "I thank God every day that He has allowed me to live in these times. Good and evil are ranged against each other in a gigantic struggle. We can be proud to take part in this battle. Now no one has a right to mediocrity." (Utrecht 2016, 327)

Conclusion

We are all called to do our part, to go out of our way to write, to read more, to arm ourselves, to speak out about the beauty of life and the inhumanity of intentionally killing others. Healthcare professionals, in particular, are called to be ministers of life and never agents of death. (John Paul II 1978, 438) We have to be like the Good Samaritan who goes over to the wounded man, pouring oil and wine on his wounds. As Pope St. John Paul II reminded us, "the person who is 'a neighbor' cannot indifferently pass by the suffering of another." (John Paul II 1984, n. 29) Von Galen did not, could not, pass by the suffering of others. What gave him such courage to speak out?

Pope Benedict XVI, in the Eucharistic celebration for the beatification of Bishop von Galen, explains.

> Where did this insight come from in a period when intelligent people seemed as if they were blind? And where did he find the strength to oppose it at a time in which even the strong proved weak and cowardly? He drew insight and courage from the faith that showed him the truth and opened his heart and his eyes.

The Lion Roars - Opposing Euthanasia

He feared God more than [human persons], and it was God who granted him the courage to do and say what others did not dare to say and do. Thus, he gives us courage, he urges us to live the faith anew today, and he also shows us how this is possible in things that are simple and humble, yet great and profound.

Let us remember that he often used to make pilgrimages on foot to the Mother of God in Telgte, that he introduced perpetual adoration at St. Servatius and that he frequently asked for the grace of forgiveness in the Sacrament of Penance and obtained it.

He therefore shows us this simple Catholicity in which the Lord meets us, in which he opens our hearts and gives us spiritual discernment, the courage of faith and the joy of being saved. Let us give thanks to God for this great witness of faith and pray to him that he will enlighten and guide us.

Blessed Cardinal von Galen, at this very moment, pray for us.... Amen. (Benedict XVI 2005)

We pray, too, for the intercession of Blessed Cardinal von Galen, the Lion of Münster. Perhaps we cannot roar quite like him, but collectively we can all raise our voices even slightly: "The lion has roared - who will not fear? The Sovereign Lord has spoken - who can but speak out?" (Amos 3:8).

Notes

1. There is no other way to do justice to such inspired sermons than to read them in full. The translation here comes from the excellent book by Fr. Daniel Utrecht (see footnote 1). Online English translations of the homilies can also be found in "Three Sermons in Defiance of the Nazis by Bishop von Galen" (available at www.churchinhistory.org/pages/booklets/vongalen(n).htm).

2. Cultural factors that erroneously support euthanasia and assisted suicide include the notion that if a life does not have a sufficient quality, then it is not worth living. A false compassion may also judge that it is better to die (or be killed) than to suffer. A third contributing factor is growing individualism where the other is viewed as a threat to one's freedom. Cf. Congregation for the Doctrine of the Faith [CDF], *Samaritanus Bonus*, Part IV: "The Cultural Obstacles that Obscure the Sacred Value of Every Human Life."

3. Cf. Benedict XVI, *Spe Salvi*, n. 22: "If technical progress is not matched by corresponding progress in [the human person's] ethical formation, in [her or his] inner growth (cf. Eph 3:16; 2 Cor 4:16), then it is not progress at all, but a threat for [humanity] and for the world."

References

Anonymous. 2021. "New Mexico Makes History Passing Innovative Bill," *Companion & Choices Magazine*, Summer.

Benedict, Pope. 2005. "Greeting of his holiness Benedict XVI at the end of the Eucharistic concelebration for the beatification of the Servant of God Cardinal Clemens August Graf von Galen." St. Peter's Basilica: October 9.

Benedict Pope. 2007. *Spe Salvi.*

Congregation for the Doctrine of the Faith (CDF). 1980. *Declaration on Euthanasia*

Congregation for the Doctrine of the Faith (CDF). 2020. *Samaritanus Bonus, letter on the care of persons in the critical and terminal phases of life.*

Flood, Bernadette. 2021. "Assisted Dying Debate Should Include Discussion of Possible Complications," *British Medical Journal* Oct 18;375: n2498.

Francis, Pope. 2013. *Evangelii Gaudium.*

Francis, Pope. 2020. Address to the participants of the Plenary Session of the Congregation for the Doctrine of the Faith. *L'Osservatore Romano.* January 30.

John Paul, Pope. 1978. Address to the Association of Italian Catholic Physicians. December 28. *Insegnamenti* I.

John Paul, Pope. 1984. *Salvifici Doloris.*

Pacholczyk, Ted. 2021. "The 'Quality of Life' Error," *Making Sense of Bioethics*. January.

Paul, Pope. 1965. *Gaudium et Spes*.

Pontifical Council for Pastoral Assistance to Health Care Workers. 2017. *New Charter for Health Care Workers* (Philadelphia, PA: National Catholic Bioethics Center). Available at https://bit.ly/3vECJYO.

Rada, Aser García. 2021. "Spain will become the sixth country worldwide to allow euthanasia and assisted suicide," *British Medical Journal* 372: n147.

Utrecht, Daniel. 2016. *The Lion of Münster: The Bishop Who Roared Against the Nazis*. Charlotte, NC: TAN Books.

HOW SHOULD MY PRACTICE OF MEDICINE BE DIFFERENT BECAUSE OF MY CATHOLIC FAITH?

Following the tradition passed on to us by the Church Fathers, the *Catechism of the Catholic Church* refers to Christ as "the physician of souls and bodies" (Catechism of the Catholic Church 1997). Jesus is the model *par excellence* of how we should live out our faith and medical practice. We should keep "our eyes fixed on Jesus" as the letter to the Hebrews exhorts us (Hebrews 12:2). Let us consider 3 P's in our Catholic medical practice - prayerful, professional, and pro-poor.

Prayerful

Jesus was very active in his ministry of healing. He cured the lepers, opened the eyes of the blind, the ears of the deaf, and even raised the dead. Here is a busy day in the life of Jesus recounted by St. Luke (Luke 4:38-40): "After he left the synagogue, he entered the house of Simon. Simon's mother-in-law was afflicted with a severe fever, and they interceded with him about her. He stood over her, rebuked the fever, and it left her. She got up immediately and waited on them. At sunset, all who had people sick with various diseases brought them to him. He laid his hands on each of them and cured them." Jesus had a hectic and busy schedule, healing and working into the late evening. What does Jesus do next? "At daybreak, Jesus left and went to a deserted place" - to pray (see Luke

4:42). Jesus drew his strength from his Father in prayer.

Learning from Jesus, the fundamental aspect of a Catholic practice of medicine is that it should be founded in prayer. Today more and more Catholics are spending some time to meditate on Scripture and be nourished by the Word of God. The *Catechism of the Catholic Church* states, "The Church 'forcefully and specifically exhorts all the Christian faithful ... to learn the "surpassing knowledge of Jesus Christ," by frequent reading of the divine Scriptures. Ignorance of the Scriptures is ignorance of Christ.'"[1]

Thus, a beautiful and fruitful way to start the day is by reading an uplifting passage from Sacred Scripture. Imagine how different a potentially busy and stressful meeting/ward round/clinic/operation would be if beforehand we were able to taste and savor an inspiring passage like Psalm 23: "The Lord is my shepherd; there is nothing I lack. In green pastures you let me graze; to safe waters you lead me; you restore my strength. You guide me along the right path for the sake of your name. Even when I walk through a dark valley, I fear no harm for you are at my side; your rod and staff give me courage" (Psalm 23:1-4). Prayer is vital, like oxygen to the soul said Padre Pio. The Church, and the hospital environment, urgently needs the "deep breath of prayer."

If a Catholic healthcare worker desires to reveal the merciful face of Christ in her work, she must first receive that mercy as a gift. Pope emeritus Benedict XVI noted astutely, "Man cannot always give love, he

How Should My Practice of Medicine Be Different Because of My Catholic Faith?

must also receive. Anyone who wishes to give love must also receive love as a gift. Certainly, as the Lord tells us, one can become a source from which rivers of living water flow. Yet to become such a source, one must constantly drink anew from the original source, which is Jesus Christ, from whose pierced heart flows the love of God." The sacraments are a most privileged place of encounter with Jesus. We vitally need that communion with Him in the Eucharist as He explains "remain united to me and you will bear much fruit, but cut off from me you can do nothing" (see John 15:4-5). Also, not only should we be obsessed with clean hands, but regular confession will help us have clean hearts, so we do not excessively contaminate others with our sinfulness.

A Catholic therefore should endeavor to develop his or her own spirituality of work and to find in it a deeper meaning and calling. How different our day, our ward, our clinic, our hospital, our healthcare system, and our world would be if we can find a minute, or two, to pray for one's patients, colleagues, and for more just healthcare systems worldwide and in this way contribute to building up the Kingdom of justice.[2]

Professional

The Second Vatican council underlined the importance of holiness for all baptized: "All Christians in any state or walk of life are called the fullness of Christian life and to the perfection of charity." Mother Teresa (1978) spoke to doctors in a Congress of the International Federation of Catholic Medical

Associations saying she wanted them "to also understand that their calling is a vocation more than a profession. A vocation is something beautiful, something holy, something great.... A doctor's vocation is very much like what Jesus did when He went about doing good and healing people." In the practice of medicine, a Catholic must work, invest all their talents, strive for excellence, and let their light shine - all for the glory of God (see Matthew 5:14-16). How wonderful it would be to see Catholic doctors, nurses, researchers, and the like forging ahead in their respective specialties, heading research teams and generally making the medical world more holy, little by little. Of course, all done with humility, remembering what St. Paul told us: "by the grace of God I am what I am" and that the greater one is, the more they should humble themselves and, in this way, find favor with God (see Sirach 3:18). It is not always easy to stay humble in medicine with all the awards and accolades of others including our patients.

It is important for Catholic healthcare professionals to be updated, not only medically but also ethically. They should strive to keep abreast of the Church's moral teachings especially regarding healthcare issues. In a booklet entitled "The Catholic Doctor / Nurse," Williams et al. (2012) note, "Confusion or failure to understand the Church's teaching in an area of faith or morals should be met with a renewed attempt to increase our knowledge of the truth." They suggest personal reading and forming study groups as specific

How Should My Practice of Medicine Be Different Because of My Catholic Faith?

ways to help inform one's faith and form one's conscience.

The formation of conscience is a challenging, ongoing, and lifelong task. Reverend Father Sabatino Majorano (1994), a Redemptorist moral theologian in Rome, and an expert on conscience and its formation writes:

> The care for the formation of the conscience clearly emerges as the fundamental ethical responsibility of every person. Whatever laziness in this regard will have immense consequences for oneself and for the others - it can never be justified. Neither is it possible at a certain point of life to stop. The path of formation needs to be continually taken up; in fact in adulthood there is a renewed responsibility in front of one's professional, family and social duties challenged by new ethical problems full of questions and uncertainties.

The Catholic healthcare professional should at least be aware of and ideally familiar with the content of the main Church documents regarding medical issues:

- *Evangelium vitae,*
- *Donum vitae,*
- *Humanae vitae,*
- *Dignitas personae,*
- Declaration on Euthanasia,
- Ethical and Religious Directives for Catholic Healthcare Services,
- Catechism of the Catholic Church.

Some key issues which Catholic healthcare workers should be well versed in, updated, and able to explain:[3]

1. To be aware of the medical/psychological/sociological consequences of abortion;

2. To be able to explain why in vitro fertilization is wrong;

3. To know the medical and moral pitfalls of contraception;

4. To be able to promote natural family planning;

5. To be updated on global trends regarding HIV infections, and familiar with the noble work the Catholic Church is doing in caring for patients with AIDS.

6. To know how to advise families on proportionate/disproportionate care;

7. To advise against physician-assisted suicide, euthanasia, and the death penalty.[4]

It may be that a Catholic, faced with opposition in the above areas, may have to exercise their prophetic ministry. A Catholic should be able to give reasons for their faith and "always be ready to give an explanation to anyone who asks you for a reason for your hope" (1 Peter 3:15). This urgency to speak prophetically is shown, for example, in the pressing need to counter the growing support for physician-assisted suicide - even the American Medical Association (AMA) is considering changing its long-held opposition. Ralph

How Should My Practice of Medicine Be Different Because of My Catholic Faith?

A. Capone (2016, 3) stated clearly, "To the agents of cultural change pressing the AMA to assume a neutral stance toward physicians who help their patients kill themselves, our response must be a resounding No!"

This is an alarming wake-up call. Many physicians, nurses, and pharmacists around the globe are increasingly realizing that it is an increasing challenge to practice medicine and also be a faithful Catholic.

Pro-poor

In medicine, it is possible to make large amounts of money and even to live a rather extravagant lifestyle. However, it should be remembered that as Catholic church, we have a so-called preferential option for the poor. Pope emeritus Benedict XVI explained it thus saying it is "natural that those who truly want to be a companion of Jesus really share in his love for the poor."[5] It does not mean the niceties of life cannot be enjoyed but within reason. Material wealth should be used wisely. The *Compendium of the Social Doctrine of the Church* reminds us that "Goods, even when legitimately owned, always have a universal destination; any type of improper accumulation is immoral" (Pontifical Council for Justice and Peace 2009). It is a very good exercise to stop once in a while and check our closets and share the extra clothes or shoes we no longer wear with those in need. The same exercise can be done with a bank account. It is not only to have the title "Catholic" (which means "universal") but to be one - a person with a universal concern for many poor brothers and sisters. It is a cause for concern if our bank account has many zeros yet many of our brothers and sisters have zero! Remember that our spirituality is also reflected in our handling of money and material goods.

Other areas to consider for economic transparency and good practice:

- Honest billing practices.
- Care should be taken in attending medical conferences. The motive should be really for academic enrichment and not just as a pretense for a holiday.
- Prudence needs to be exercised in relations with the pharmaceutical industry, their products, and their representatives. Some doctors, influenced by favors received from a pharmaceutical company, too readily prescribe their treatments/products.
- If a Catholic healthcare worker receives gifts that are too lavish, he or she may become overindebted to the giver: as Dr Hai Thuong Lan Ong (the founder of Vietnamese medical ethics) once warned "recipients of [lavish] gifts often become subservient" (Hoa Trung Dinh 2016).

If we have considered some aspects of material wealth and poverty, we should not forget spiritual poverty. Who of us does not at some point feel sad, lonely, discouraged, hopeless and in need of encouragement, consolation, support, a listening ear, a kind word? In the workplace, a wonderful way to evangelize is to begin with a smile and to greet those around us, from the janitor down to our bosses. Even to ask a person, "how are you?" is a simple yet wonderful way to live out mission in the workplace: "As Catholic physicians, nurses and healthcare professionals we are in a unique position to evangelize a number of individuals on a daily basis. We are 'missionary disciples' and have multiple opportunities to live and share our faith not only through our words but more importantly through our actions" (Catholic Medical Association 2016).

Conclusion

To be able to encounter the face of Christ in every sick person is an undeserved privilege. When I touch a patient, I am touching Christ himself as we hear in chapter 25 of Matthew's gospel: "I was ill and you cared for me" (Matthew 25:36). To practice medicine as a Catholic is ultimately a vocation and a personal response to the love of Christ. This is what our Lord asks for - our personal response. After asking his disciples the opinion of the crowds, he then asks them, and each one us, "But who do you say that I am?" (Mark 8:29). The challenge will be each day to do it for Him as the letter to the Colossians reminds us, "Whatever you do, do from the heart, as for the Lord" (Colossians 3:23).

There is no doubt that a Catholic healthcare worker can do much good in the medical world of today. Fr. Jaime Bonet, the founder of the *Fraternidad Misionera Verbum Dei* community, stated that as the injection in the vein of the arm strengthens the entire body, so the life that passes through only one soul heals the whole Church. We can all strive to be faithful in the small, and our Lord will take care of the rest. Whatever we do, we should try to do it well as Cardinal Newman (1848) prayed, "God has created me to do Him some definite service; He has committed some work to me which He has not committed to another." May the Virgin Mary inspire us more and more each day to make our practice of medicine, little by little, more Catholic.

Notes

1. *Catechism of the Catholic Church* (1997), n. 133. Citing *Dei verbum*, n. 25; cf. Phil 3:8 and St. Jerome, *Commentariorum in Isaiam libri* xviii prol.: PL 24,17B.

2. Intercessory prayer has a power of its own. Pope Pius XII wrote, "This is a deep mystery, and an inexhaustible subject of meditation, that the salvation of many depends on the prayers and voluntary penances which the members of the Mystical Body of Jesus Christ offer" in *Mystici Corporis Christi*, n. 44.

3. Some elements were already mentioned but their importance permits a slight repetition.

4. Pope Francis, together with the worldwide Bishops, stated emphatically that the Church "firmly rejects the death penalty." *Relatio finalis*, XIV Ordinary General Assembly of the Synod of Bishops (October 24, 2015), n. 64, quoted in *Amoris Laetitia*, n. 83.

5. Pope emeritus Benedict XVI, Address to Fathers of the General Congregation of the Society of Jesus, Thursday, February 21, 2008.

How Should My Practice of Medicine Be Different Because of My Catholic Faith?

References

Benedict, Pope. 2005. *Deus Caritas Est*, n. 7.

Capone, Ralph A. 2016, October. "AMA Reconsiders Opposition to Physician-assisted Suicide," *Ethics & Medics* 41, n. 10: 1-3.

Catechism of the Catholic Church. 1997. United States Conference of Catholic Bishops, 2nd ed. Vatican City: Libreria Editrice Vaticana, n. 1509.

Catholic Medical Association. *Virtuous Medicine: The Joy and Privilege of the Catholic Physician*.

Francis, Pope. 2013. *Evangelii Gaudium*, n. 232.

Hoa Trung Dinh, S. J. 2016. "Yi-Dao: The Dao of Medicine in the Works of Hai Thuong Lan Ong." In *Doing Asian Theological Ethics in a Cross-cultural and an Interreligious Context*, edited by F. James Yiu, Sing Lúcás Chan, and Shaji George Kochuthara, 329. Bangalore, India: Dharmaram.

Majorano, S., Fr. 1994. *La Coscienza*. Torino, Italy: Edizioni San Paolo, 182.

Newman, Cardinal John Henry. 1848. "Meditations on Christian Doctrine," *Hope in God - Creator*, March 7.

Pontifical Council for Justice and Peace. 2009. *Compendium of the Social Doctrine of the Church*, n. 328. London, UK: Libreria Editrice Vaticana.

Second Vatican council, *Lumen Gentium*, n. 31.

Teresa, Mother M. 1978. "My work in India." Proceedings of the XIV World Congress of the International Federation of Catholic Medical Associations (FIAMC), Quality of Life in a Changing Society, Bombay, India, January 29 to February 1, 1978.

Williams, Anne-Marie, Treloar Adrian, Treloar Josephine, Doogan Mary, and O'Sullivan John-Paul. 2012, February. "The Catholic Doctor/Nurse," *Catholic Medical Quarterly* 62, n. 1: 10-11.

WHY THE CHURCH SAYS "YES" TO LIFE AND "NO" TO IVF

Summary

This article presents the principal Church teachings regarding in vitro fertilization (IVF). Since the birth of Louise Brown, the world's first "test-tube" baby in 1978, around eight million IVF babies have been born. The Magisterium has pronounced her main teachings on IVF in Donum Vitae (1987), Evangelium Vitae (1995), and Dignitas Personae (2008). The Church says "no" to IVF due to the massive destruction of embryonic life, the assault on the meaning of the conjugal act and the treatment of the child as a product not a gift. She continues to announce a loud "yes" to life, endeavoring to take care of the human embryo, the least of our brothers and sisters (see Matthew 25:40).

The Church, as Mother, shows great concern for those couples who suffer from infertility. "Couples who discover that they are sterile suffer greatly. 'What will you give me,' asks Abraham of God, 'for I continue childless?' and Rachel cries to her husband Jacob, 'Give me children, or I shall die!'" (Catechism of the Catholic Church 1997, n. 2374). She also encourages ethical research that aims to prevent and treat infertility (Catechism of the Catholic Church 1997, n. 2375). However, the Church also has a sacred duty to defend human life, and to speak out whenever it is threatened or in danger. A controversial area nowadays is when the infertile couple wishes to resort to in vitro fertilization (IVF). Once a religious Sister asked me, "If God is a God of life, why does the Church say 'no' to IVF?" This question can serve as a springboard to enter into a review of Church teaching on the topic of IVF. We will look at the main teachings on the subject from her Magisterium, and see how the Church gives a big "yes" to life, a big "no" to IVF and the reasons why.

The first specific Magisterial pronouncement on IVF came with the release of *Donum Vitae*, an instruction on respect for human life in its origin and on the dignity of procreation, issued 22 February 1987, by the Congregation for the Doctrine of the Faith (Congregation for the Doctrine of the Faith 1987). This was 9 years after the birth of Louise Brown in England, the world's first "test-tube" baby in 1978. *Donum Vitae* reiterated some fundamental concepts of Catholic teaching, such as the dignity of the person and the respect due human life from the moment of conception. The Instruction also noted that the technique of IVF involved wanton destruction of human embryonic life. It also taught the important principle that only techniques that assist the conjugal act were licit, not those that replace it.

Donum Vitae also addressed the suffering caused by infertility in marriage. "The suffering of spouses who cannot have children ... is a suffering that everyone must understand and properly evaluate"

Why the Church Says "Yes" to Life and "No" to IVF

(Congregation for the Doctrine of the Faith 1987, II.8). The document underlines that sterility is a difficult trial and encourages research to alleviate this burden:

> "Scientists therefore are to be encouraged to continue their research with the aim of preventing the causes of sterility and of being able to remedy them so that sterile couples will be able to procreate in full respect for their own personal dignity and that of the child to be born" (Congregation for the Doctrine of the Faith 1987, II.8).

The next milestone in Catholic teaching came with Pope John Paul II's *Evangelium Vitae* in 1995. His charter on the Gospel of Life dealt with a wide range of issues at the beginning of life (such as population concerns, contraception, sterilization and abortion) and at the end of life (such as euthanasia and the death penalty), among others. Regarding IVF and related techniques, we find in number 14:

> The various techniques of artificial reproduction, which would seem to be at the service of life and which are frequently used with this intention, actually open the door to new threats against life. Apart from the fact that they are morally unacceptable, since they separate procreation from the fully human context of the conjugal act, these techniques have a high rate of failure: not just failure in relation to fertilization but with regard to the subsequent development of the embryo, which

is exposed to the risk of death, generally within a very short space of time. Furthermore, the number of embryos produced is often greater than that needed for implantation in the woman's womb, and these so-called "spare embryos" are then destroyed or used for research which, under the pretext of scientific or medical progress, in fact reduces human life to the level of simple "biological material" to be freely disposed of (John Paul II 1995, n. 14).

On 8 September 2008, the Feast of the Nativity of the Blessed Virgin Mary, the Congregation for the Doctrine of the Faith released *Dignitas Personae* on certain bioethical questions (Congregation for the Doctrine of the Faith 2008). Seeing as this is the latest pronouncement on the technique of IVF, we will look at this document more closely. Dignitas Personae points out:

- Around a third of women who seek recourse to IVF eventually succeed in having a baby (n. 14).

- The number of embryos sacrificed is extremely high - those with defects are discarded; if too many implant successfully in the uterus, they are then selectively reduced (= aborted), and other embryos will be lost in the freezing/thawing procedures (n. 14).

- in vitro fertilization creates an ethically unacceptable dissociation of procreation from the integrally personal context of the conjugal act (n. 16).

Why the Church Says "Yes" to Life and "No" to IVF

- The legitimate desire for a child and the suffering of the parents struggling with infertility cannot justify the "production" of offspring (n. 16).

- Research and investment directed at the prevention of sterility deserve encouragement (n. 13).[1]

The one area which continues to be cloudy is what to do with the ever-increasing number of frozen embryos languishing in clinics?[2] These excess embryos are created to avoid repeated rounds of harvesting and fertilization. However, the "little souls," frozen on ice (liquid nitrogen), are left to face an unsolvable situation. What to do with them? Rescue and adopt them? Or is this just giving a big thumbs up to the whole IVF industry? Leave them on ice? Let them thaw and die? When the United Kingdom announced that 3300 embryos were to be discarded (having passed the limit of 5 years of storage), a group of 200 women banded together in Italy and requested to prenatally adopt these embryos (Demartis 1998). Even some nuns asked the Vatican if they could offer their wombs to rescue these frozen little ones!

Regarding the fate of the millions of frozen embryos in storage, *Dignitas Personae* stresses that this is "*a situation of injustice which in fact cannot be resolved*" (Congregation for the Doctrine of the Faith 2008, n. 19). Much has subsequently been written on the debate regarding the moral fate of these little ones, but to date, there still has been no specific Magisterial teaching on this challenging topic.

With these three documents, *Donum Vitae* (1987), *Evangelium Vitae* (1995), and *Dignitas Personae* (2008), the Church has laid out her teaching clearly. She wishes to continue to shout a big "yes" to life and defend against any practices which threaten or destroy human life. In summary then, her main reasons for saying "no" to IVF are:

The Massive Destruction of Human Life

The IVF industry involves massive destruction of human life. For each live baby produced, many of its brother and sister embryos are destroyed in the process. *Dignitas Personae* tells us that even in the best centers up to 80% of embryos are lost or destroyed (Congregation for the Doctrine of the Faith 2008, footnote 27).

The separation of the unitive and procreative dimensions of the conjugal act

These two dimensions, union and procreation, more simply remembered as bonding and babies, are two inseparable aspects of the sexual act. *Humanae Vitae* (1968) had already clearly underlined this, "the inseparable connection, established by God, which man on his own initiative may not break, between the unitive significance and the procreative significance which are both inherent to the marriage act" (Paul VI 1968, n. 12).

Why the Church Says "Yes" to Life and "No" to IVF

The Child is a Gift, not a Manufacturing Product

The child has the right "to be the fruit of the specific act of the conjugal love of his parents" (Catechism of the Catholic Church 1997, n. 2378). Mother Church reminds us that, "In reality, the origin of a human person is the result of an act of giving. The one conceived must be the fruit of his parents' love. He cannot be desired or conceived as the product of an intervention of medical or biological techniques; that would be equivalent to reducing him to an object of scientific technology. No one may subject the coming of a child into the world to conditions of technical efficiency which are to be evaluated according to standards of control and dominion" (Congregation for the Doctrine of the Faith 1987, II, 4a).

Teaching of Pope Francis

In addition to these documents mentioned above from the Magisterium, Pope Francis has written on the need to uphold ethical principles when dealing with life issues. In *Laudato Si'*, his document on the care of the environment, he cautions that "when technology disregards the great ethical principles, it ends up considering any practice whatsoever as licit" (Francis 2015, n. 136). In the same document, speaking of the human embryo, he asks "How can we genuinely teach the importance of concern for other vulnerable beings, however troublesome or inconvenient they may be, if we fail to protect a human embryo?" (Francis 2015, n. 120).

In *Amoris Laetitia*, a document more specifically about love in the family, in number 56, the Pontiff makes a specific reference to assisted reproductive techniques writing:

> The technological revolution in the field of human procreation has introduced the ability to manipulate the reproductive act, making it independent of the sexual relationship between a man and a woman. In this way, human life and parenthood have become modular and separable realities, subject mainly to the wishes of individuals or couples. It is one thing to be understanding of human weakness and the complexities of life, and another to accept ideologies that attempt to sunder what are inseparable aspects of reality. Let us not fall into the sin of trying to replace the Creator. We are creatures, and not omnipotent. Creation is prior to us and must be received as a gift. At the same time, we are called to protect our humanity, and this means, in the first place, accepting it and respecting it as it was created (Francis 2016, n. 56).

Aside from these teachings from the Magisterium, the respective Bishops' Conferences in each country, and the local Catholic Medical Associations, often offer helpful explanations of Church teaching on IVF.

Conclusion

With over eight million live births since the technique was introduced in 1978, IVF has become a "normal"

Why the Church Says "Yes" to Life and "No" to IVF

way to treat infertility.[3] However, there are clearly very troubling aspects of the procedure, clearly taught by the Church's Magisterium and outlined above, especially the massive destruction of embryonic life, the assault on the meaning of the conjugal act and the treatment of the child as a product not a gift. The Catholic Church clearly states that IVF should not be practiced. What is worrying is that most Catholics (some healthcare workers, lay, priests and religious included) may know the Church says "no" but unfortunately cannot give any reasons or explain the *why*. Hopefully, this article can contribute in its own little way to redress this anomaly somewhat.

The Church as Mother identifies with the suffering caused by infertility. In her pronouncements she seeks to express that closeness to the infertile couple, as well as animating and encouraging sound ethical research to seek solutions. This is clearly seen for example in the address of Pope John Paul II to the Pontifical Academy for Life: "Consequently, I would like to encourage scientific research that seeks a natural way to overcome the infertility of the spouses, and likewise to urge all specialists to perfect those procedures that can serve this end" (John Paul II 2004, n. 3).

The Church continues to shout a loud "yes" to life, and each one of us is called to add our voice to this chorus. In doing so, we strive to uphold the dignity of the human embryo, the smallest of our brothers and sisters, remembering the words of our Lord, "Whatever you do to the least of these brothers and sisters of mine, you did it to me" (Matthew 25:40).

Notes

1. Research is aimed at prevention of infertility, also seeking to elucidate and possibly remedy any causative factors. In the female for example, if the fallopian tubes are blocked, corrective surgery may be feasible. At times, the couple can be helped by learning about the natural biological rhythms of fertility, through programs of natural family planning. In this regard, Natural Procreative Technology (NaProTechnology), where available, is an acceptable approach to infertility therapy according to Catholic teachings.

2. There are estimated to be at least 1 million frozen embryos in the United States alone.

3. It should also be remembered that in front of an existing IVF birth the Church teaches that "although the manner in which human conception is achieved with IVF and ET cannot be approved, every child which comes into the world must in any case be accepted as a living gift of the divine Goodness and must be brought up with love" (Congregation for the Doctrine of the Faith 1987, II, B5).

References

Congregation for the Doctrine of the Faith (1987) *Donum Vitae*, Instruction on Respect for Human Life in Its Origin and on the Dignity of Procreation.

Why the Church Says "Yes" to Life and "No" to IVF

Congregation for the Doctrine of the Faith (2008) *Dignitas Personae*, Instruction on Certain Bioethical Questions.

Demartis, Francesco (1998) "Mass Pre-Embryo Adoption." *Cambridge Quarterly of Healthcare Ethics* 7(1): 101-103. DOI: 10.1017/ S0963180198701136.

Francis, Pope. 2015. *Laudato Si'*.

Francis, Pope. 2016. *Amoris Laetitia*.

John Paul, Pope, II. 1995. *Evangelium Vitae*.

John Paul, Pope, II (2004) *Address of John Paul II to the Members of the Pontifical Academy for Life*.

Paul, Pope VI. 1968. *Humanae Vitae*.

INTERNET PORNOGRAPHY: SOME MEDICAL AND SPIRITUAL PERSPECTIVES

Summary

The Internet has made pornography available on a massive scale. Data released by "Pornhub" the world's most popular Internet porn site, reveal that in 2019 alone, there were over 42 billion visits to its website, which in itself is an incredible waste of time and energy, which could be more fruitfully employed. Pornography viewing is poisonous for the conscience and commodifies the human body, reducing it to an object of abusive pleasure. Its negative effects can be broadly seen in three overlapping categories: personal, psychological, and social. The antidote is a renewed call to chastity, that self-mastery that can help direct one's passions in a more fruitful way. Without prayer, we cannot live chastely as "the spirit is willing but the flesh is weak" (Matthew 26:41). There is an urgency for the new evangelization to help recapture the dignity of the body and counter the lie of pornography, and to ensure that in the digital world, the face of Christ needs to be seen and his voice heard.

The first time I was consulted regarding issues pertaining to Internet pornography was around ten years ago. A young woman in her early thirties approached me as a moral theologian to ask for some advice. She had become caught up in pornography, met someone online, and was now entering into the initial stages of cybersex. To be honest, I was a little

Internet Pornography:
Some Medical and Spiritual Perspectives

shell-shocked after our dialogue. I was not really updated on pornography, and my own recalling was limited to a color print magazine I once saw in my younger days in a barber's shop. I cautiously began investigating the topic of Internet pornography, reading Church teachings, and dialoging with other missionaries who were also engaged in the apostolate. We began to grasp that Internet pornography is a whole new ball game.

We realized that the issue was hidden, but growing, and decided to offer a formation to our lay people who were asking about it. I had actually given the previous formation on conscience, so as we take turns, the priests were quite relieved that it now fell to our Sisters to give the topic. One Sister bravely decided to give the formation, if I would also help in the preparations. When it came to the publicity, a Spanish missionary caught the attention of all when he announced that "Sister will be giving a pornographic formation." I had to gently inform him that in English it is better to say that "Sister will be giving us a formation on pornography."

The first formation was attended by fifty interested lay people of all ages. One grandmother, slightly hard of hearing, caused a stir as every so often she would stand up, notebook in hand, and ask Sister to repeat certain phrases. The grandma explained, "I have to get the quotes exact because I am going to share them with my neighbors!" The formation went well, and we even got some questions in the "Q and A" section although we began to notice that most interventions were never in first person narrative but began with the phrase "I have a friend who ..."

Overview of the Medical Literature

There are various caveats to bear in mind when viewing the issue of Internet pornography solely through a medical and/or psychological lens. Being a relatively new phenomenon - the Internet came to be in the early 1990s - there is still much to learn, and research to be done. Some considerations include:

1. Problematic use of pornography or pornography addiction do not yet appear as diagnostic categories in the *Diagnostic and Statistical Manual of Mental Disorders* (DSM-5) of the American Psychiatric Association (2013). However, with the inclusion of gambling disorder in *DSM-5*, there is the formal recognition that various behaviors can be classified as addictions with Internet gaming disorder also earmarked as a "Condition for further study." We will return to the theme of the "addictiveness" of pornography at various points in this essay.

2. There is no consensus to date on what constitutes a definition of pornography. Peter and Valkenberg (2016), in their review of twenty years of research on pornography, define it as "professionally produced or user-generated pictures or videos (clips) intended to sexually arouse the viewer" (p. 509). Dr. Peter Kleponis (2019), a leading expert in pornography addiction recovery, defines pornography as "any image that leads a person to use another person for his or her own sexual pleasure. It is devoid of love,

intimacy, relationship, or responsibility. It can be highly addictive" (p. 21).

3. Clinicians have not yet agreed on what constitutes problematic or addictive behavior. Various proposals are discussed in the literature in answer to the question "When does the use of Internet pornography become pathological?"

4. Reviewing the medical literature yields little helpful practical information for treatment options. Various pharmacological approaches (such as using paroxetine or naltrexone) and psychotherapeutic interventions (such as cognitive behavioral therapy) have been tried with varied results (see treatment options in the review of Sniewski, Farvida, and Carter 2018).

There are limits to an approach that views the issue through the singular lens of medicine, in an exclusive and limited way. Some authors will even conclude that Internet pornography is not such a bad thing after all, as the provocatively titled article of Fisher and Kohut suggests, "Pornography Viewing: Keep Calm and Carry On" (Fisher and Kohut, 2017, 320). Part of their advice is indeed helpful - "we need to step back from the media hype, recognize that the evidence concerning pornography harms is often inconsistent or flawed, and read research reports carefully and critically" (Fisher and Kohut 2017, 321). However, inviting viewers of pornography, many of whom are adolescents, to "keep calm and carry on" watching is inexpedient. The title of their article is misleading and such a laissez-faire attitude will continue to lead many impressionable minds astray. Fisher and Kohut write "from a clinical perspective, we need keep eternally open minds" (321), but this needs to be nuanced with a real note of caution. The authors seem rather naive in their underestimation of the dangers of porn.

We receive additional light on such dangers when we add a Catholic theological analysis to our somewhat limited medical perspective. Medicine, and psychology/psychiatry do not have a monopoly over the field of human knowledge. Researchers and clinicians in the field of Internet pornography would do well to integrate perspectives from others sciences such as Catholic moral theology, where categories such as prayer, spirituality, grace, and sin can give additional insights, resulting in a more holistic and comprehensive view of the issue.

In this essay, I will also draw from experiences of dialogues and interviews with persons who have sought advice regarding their difficulties in the area of excessive pornography consumption. The Catholic church values human experience as a category of analysis when examining the morality of certain issues. We see this clearly in the document *Gaudium et Spes*, a conciliar document from the authoritative Second Vatican Council, which states that the pressing issues of the age can be considered "in the light of the Gospel and of human experience" (Vatican Council II 1965, n. 46).

Internet Pornography:
Some Medical and Spiritual Perspectives

Online Pornography Is Trending

Dwulit and Rzymski report that "due to a high sense of anonymity and almost unrestricted access, the Internet has become the most important medium of dissemination of pornographic content (known as online pornography), particularly in the form of images and videos" (Dwulit and Rzymski, 2019, 914). Data released by "Pornhub," the world's most popular Internet porn site, reveal that in 2019 alone, there were over 42 billion visits to its website (Pornhub 2019).[1] If you started watching all the new videos (just uploaded in 2019), you would finish in the year 2188. But by November 2022, the number of visits to the top three internet porn sites had grown to approximately 24 billion visits per month! The following data can help us grasp the staggering extent of the problem:

> About 200,000 Americans are classified as "porn addicts." (Webroot n.d.)
>
> 40 million American people regularly visit porn sites.
>
> 35% of all internet downloads are related to pornography.
>
> 34% of internet users have experienced unwanted exposure to pornographic content through ads, pop up ads, misdirected links or emails.
>
> One-third of porn viewers are women.

Of course, being a global issue, the effects of pornography reach the four corners of the globe. As the Filipino Bishops note:

> Given the all-pervasiveness of the Internet, it should not be surprising that pornography has invaded our homes, workplaces, schools, and churches. The Young Adult Fertility and Sexuality (YAFS) Study of Filipino Youth in 2013 has revealed that 56.5% of Filipinos aged 15 to 24 years old have been exposed to pornographic videos and movies, 35.6% have been exposed to sexually explicit reading materials, and 15.5% have viewed pornographic websites. These young people are the future husbands and wives, fathers and mothers, of our nation, whose capacity for self-giving love has been deeply wounded. (Catholic Bishops' Conference of the Philippines 2016)

Negative Effects of Pornography

There are ongoing debates within the medical literature about whether Internet pornography use is addictive or not, with some arguing that it is inherently addictive, others mostly innocuous or simply understudied. Grubbs and Perry note that "while these debates continue, there is clear evidence that some people do find their own use of pornography to be problematic" (Grubbs and Perry 2019, 29). They also specify "at present, there is simply no consensus within either sexual research or addiction research fields as to

Internet Pornography:
Some Medical and Spiritual Perspectives

whether pornography use can be an addictive activity in and of itself" (Grubbs and Perry 2019, 30). Bearing in mind this declaration, it does not mean we cannot say anything about the wrongfulness of pornography. Addiction is not the sole and exclusive marker of the inherent wrongfulness of an activity. The *Catechism of the Catholic Church* clearly and synthetically explains the implicit moral wrongness of pornography. It teaches:

> Pornography consists in removing real or simulated sexual acts from the intimacy of the partners, in order to display them deliberately to third parties. It offends against chastity because it perverts the conjugal act, the intimate giving of spouses to each other. It does grave injury to the dignity of its participants (actors, vendors, the public), since each one becomes an object of base pleasure and illicit profit for others. It immerses all who are involved in the illusion of a fantasy world. It is a grave offense. Civil authorities should prevent the production and distribution of pornographic materials. (Catechism of the Catholic Church 1997, n. 2354)

There are various ways proposed to evaluate the negative consequences of pornography. Sniewski, Farvida, and Carter refer to problematic pornography consumption as "any use of pornography that leads to and/or produces significant negative inter-personal, vocational, or personal consequences for the user" (Sniewski, Farvida, and Carter 2018, 217). These same authors report "an individual can experience pornography use as problematic for a myriad of reasons. These include personal or moral, social and relationship, time spent viewing, or viewing in inappropriate contexts such as at work" (Sniewski, Farvida, and Carter 2018, 218). For our own purposes, I will summarize here the negative effects of pornography in three broad and overlap- ping categories: personal, psychological, and social (especially regarding marriage and family).

Personal Dangers

A young man, twenty years old, commented to me, "Father, I have been watching porn since I was ten years old. There is nothing I have not seen. Some images will stay with me the rest of my life." I did not inquire further as to what he had seen![2]

I have met people who claim that pornography viewing is not harmful because it is something done "in private." This is slightly naive and shows a lack of full comprehension of human action. As social beings, our actions always have social repercussions. The *Catechism of the Catholic Church* has noted that pornography "does grave injury to the dignity of its participants" (Catechism of the Catholic Church 1997, n. 2354) especially to the actors and actresses who may be victims of sex trafficking, and performing against their will, in what is termed "coerced pornography."

Furthermore, to consider that pornography is not harmful is to underestimate one's opponent - usually a fatal mistake in warfare. An interesting "parable"

Internet Pornography:
Some Medical and Spiritual Perspectives

highlights the nature of the beast. One day a boy met a poisonous snake at the bottom of a hill. The boy wanted to climb the hill and the snake begged the boy to carry him. The boy objected that the snake would bite him. "Of course, I won't" retorted the snake, "I am your friend," and he managed to convince the boy to carry him. The boy carried the snake with him to the top of the hill. Thereupon the snake announced, "See I did not bite you, I am your friend, please carry me back down." The boy carried the poisonous snake down the hill. At the bottom of the hill, the snake asked to be put down. On the ground, the snake saw the bare ankle of the boy and lunged at him, sinking its fangs deep into the boy's leg filling him with venom. The boy cried out in agony and wailed "Why did you bite me? I thought you were my friend?" The snake hissed, "I am a snake. A snake is a snake. And a snake bites."

Pornography viewing has a bite. The viewing of pornography is sinful, not only incurring the sin of lust but also encroaching on the sins of laziness and omission because of the precious time and valuable energy wasted which otherwise could be more gainfully employed. Viewing porn poisons the conscience and makes it quasi-impossible to keep a clean gaze, especially when looking at the body of the other. St Matthew's Gospel has some pertinent words for us, "The lamp of the body is the eye. It follows that if your eye is clear, your whole body will be filled with light. But if your eye is diseased, your whole body will be darkness" (Matthew 6:22). Often when people come to me for advice about a sexual vice, like excessive masturbation or marital infidelity, they share that they feel their sexual desires are out of control. I usually inquire about viewing of pornography, as a principal background driving factor, because the fire of sexual desire will become out of control, and hard to manage, if one is frequently pouring the "gasoline" of pornography onto it.

The personal dangers may be exacerbated when pornography is viewed at a younger age. In a review titled "The Impact of Internet Pornography on Adolescents: A Review of the Research," Owens et al. note the consistent findings emerging "linking adolescent use of pornography that depicts violence with increased degrees of sexually aggressive behavior." They underline that "girls report feeling physically inferior to the women they view in pornographic material, while boys fear they may not be as virile or able to perform as the men in these media" (Owens et al. 2012, 116). They also note that "adolescents who use pornography, especially that found on the Internet, have lower degrees of social integration, increases in conduct problems, higher levels of delinquent behavior, higher incidence of depressive symptoms, and decreased emotional bonding with caregivers" (Owens et al. 2012, 116).

Psychological: The Addiction Spiral

There is strong neuroscientific evidence for the potentially addictive nature of Internet pornography (Love et al. 2015, 413).[3] Some anti-porn groups label

Internet Pornography:
Some Medical and Spiritual Perspectives

pornography as the new drug. Like most drugs, it can easily trap the user. In considering pornography as a drug, a brief consideration of the specific neuronal reward pathways and involved hormones is merited. Dr. Peter Kleponis, in his excellent book *Integrity Restored: Helping Catholic Families Win the Battle against Pornography* (Revised and Expanded Edition) succinctly summarizes what could otherwise be a complex area. The thalamus, a small structure situated above the brain stem, has a particular role in identifying sexual images, such that "if a man is viewing a hundred different images and one of them is erotic, the thalamus is going to help him single it out, and the man will immediately pay attention to the erotic image" (Kleponis 2019, 43). The main hormones involved in the masculine sexual response to viewing porn are dopamine (released particularly from the ventral tegmental area of the midbrain) which mixes with testosterone to create a sense of excitement. Added in are norepinephrine to stimulate the body, Delta Fos-B to fuel more cravings for porn, and vasopressin to bond the man to his computer screen. Ensuing masturbation releases euphoria-inducing endorphins at orgasm. So, we have dopamine, testosterone, norepinephrine, Delta Fos-B (also known as iFos-B), vasopressin, and opiate chemicals (endorphins) - quite a potent cocktail overall!

The following steps can often be observed in the gradual downward spiral of excessive use of Internet pornography: discovery, experimentation, habituation, compulsivity.

JESUS THE DIVINE PHYSICIAN

Discovery: Many first-time users stumble on explicit online images or videos by chance. Alternatively, they may be introduced to them by a friend. At the beginning, curiosity is aroused by viewing such images. This is the discovery stage. We note alarmingly that the average age for first watching porn is just eight years old (Kleponis 2019, 108).

Experimentation: There is so much pornography available on line. Typing "porn" alone on your Google search engine will give you 939 million hits. That's a lot of material for the curious. Curiosity not only killed the cat but also led to the downfall of King David. "One evening David rose from his bed and strolled about on the roof of the king's house. From the roof he saw a woman bathing; she was very beautiful. David sent people to inquire about the woman …" (2 Samuel 11:2-3). With a superabundance of available porn, and of all varieties, the curious user can easily enter into a stage of experimentation. This phase is reinforced by the concomitant masturbation that predictably accompanies watching porn. Orgasm is a powerful stimulus to search for more.

Habituation: Most drugs need increasingly higher doses to get the same high. Should users continue their pornographic quest, tolerance to mild images may develop such that the person becomes habituated. Kleponis explains an underlying mechanism: "After the orgasm, there is a period of intense relaxation. Then the 'crash' occurs. The high levels of dopamine drop dramatically, creating a 'dopamine hangover'. Symptoms of this can include irritability, depression,

Internet Pornography:
Some Medical and Spiritual Perspectives

and anxiety. Not liking the dopamine hangover, the brain will try to escape it" (Kleponis 2019, 44). The man will then have to go back to pornography to get a new fix and a new high.

Stronger images may soon be required such that scenes such as sexual violence, which formerly caused repulsion and disgust, may become more and more "normal." In discussing "the development of habituation to previous stimuli" de Alarcón et al. underline the "dysfunctional enhanced preference for sexual novelty, which may manifest as attempts to overcome said habituation and desensitization through the search for more (new) pornography as a means of sexual satisfaction, choosing this behavior instead of actual sex" (de Alarcón et al., 2019, 8). As the bad habit progresses, the vitiated behavior becomes a "vice" and starts to exert a vice-like grip on the consumer who becomes progressively hooked.

Compulsivity. Men using pornography found "the way they looked at women in real life warping to fit the pornography fantasies they consumed onscreen. It wasn't only their sex lives that suffered - pornography's effects rippled out, touching all aspects of their existence. Their work days became interrupted, their hobbies were tossed aside, their family lives were disrupted. Some men even lost their jobs, their wives, and their children. The sacrifice is enormous" (Eberstadt and Layden 2010, 39). The compulsivity can become destructive and out of control. "When the viewing of pornography rises to the level of addiction, 40 percent of 'sex addicts' lose their spouses, 58 percent suffer considerable financial losses, and about a third lose their jobs" (Fagan 2009, 7).

Accurate "addiction" rates are hard to come by as not all may admit their problematic issue. In a Spanish survey of 2,408 Internet users, one-third experienced negative consequences from pornography use in their family, social, academic, or work environment (Villena, Contreras, and Chiclana 2017, e254). In a study of 20,094 participants in Australia, 4.4 percent of men and 1.2 percent of women reported that they were addicted to pornography (Rissel et al. 2016, 221). In another study from Germany, 3 percent of women had problems with pornography use (Baranowski, Vogl, and Stark 2019, 1274). A principal reason for a woman's entanglement in porn is a craving for intimacy (Kleponis 2019, 77). The woman, who may even be married, lacks a deeper connectedness. For women, the relationship is key - if a man is visually stimulated, the women is relationally stimulated. For her, the pornographic imaginations can be provoked by words. This helps explain why women are usually more interested in "forms of pornography that promise relational connection and romance, such as erotic literature or inappropriate social media interactions and video chats" (US Conference of Catholic Bishops 2015, 12). The danger is that in her frantic pursuit of relationship, the online virtual sexual frolicking can easily transition to an actual meet up and later inappropriate real-life sexual relationships in a desperate search for intimacy.

Internet Pornography:
Some Medical and Spiritual Perspectives

The risk of problematic use of Internet porn is compounded by what is known as the "triple A" influence - accessibility of Internet nowadays, affordability in that the cost of an Internet connection is within the reach of most people, and complete anonymity can be offered (de Alarcón et al. 2019, 1). de Alarcón et al. also give a list of indicative risk factors for pornography use. Predictors for problematic sexual behavior and pornography use are, across populations: being a man, young age, religiousness, frequent Internet use, negative mood states, and being prone to sexual boredom and novelty seeking (de Alarcón et al 2019, 4). What is not yet defined is when problematic online pornography use becomes pathological, but indicative features from various researchers may include elements of "loss of control, excessive time spent on sexual behavior and negative consequences to self and others" (de Alarcón et al. 2019, 12).

Self-perceived problematic porn use refers to "an individual who self-identifies as addicted to porn because they feel they are unable to regulate their porn consumption, and that use interferes with everyday life" (Sniewski, Farvida, and Carter 2018, 218). Reviewing the available literature, Sniewski, Farvida, and Carter report that problematic pornography use has been quantified as: spending at least eleven hours per week viewing pornography, consuming daily, or surpassing a threshold of seven orgasms per week. Around 9 percent of porn consumers fulfill these criteria (Sniewski, Farvida, and Carter 2018, 220). It should be noted however that "self-diagnoses may not always reflect severe dysregulation or compulsivity. However, they almost invariably do represent an important threat to mental health, relational functioning, and general well-being" (Grubbs and Perry 2019, 33). We have noted that there is an ongoing debate about the addictive potential of Internet pornography. Grubbs and Perry (2019) point out that "people often self-identify as addicted to pornography, even when the mental health and psychiatric communities have not officially recognized the diagnosis" (p. 31). Thus, the concept of "perceived addiction to Internet pornography" may be helpful also.

Social Effects

Various studies are now reporting the hazardous effects of pornography. Dr. Patrick Fagan of the Family Research Council reports that (Executive summary):

- Married men who are involved in pornography feel less satisfied with their conjugal relations and less emotionally attached to their wives.
- Wives notice and are upset by the difference. Pornography use is also a pathway to infidelity and divorce and is frequently a major fac- tor in these family disasters.
- Among couples affected by one spouse's addiction, two-thirds experience a loss of interest in sexual intercourse.
- Both spouses perceive pornography viewing as tantamount to infidelity.

Internet Pornography:
Some Medical and Spiritual Perspectives

- Pornography viewing leads to a loss of interest in good family relations. (Fagan 2009)

The Filipino Bishops note that "empirical studies have shown that prolonged exposure to pornography in young people ... is also correlated with high-risk sexual behaviors that put them at peril for sexually transmitted diseases" (Catholic Bishops' Conference of the Philippines 2016). The viewing of Internet pornography damages sexual identity and can affect sexual behavior. There is strong empirical data to support this, such as a Dutch study of adolescents, where the authors found "that more frequent exposure to sexually explicit Internet material is associated with greater sexual uncertainty and more positive attitudes toward uncommitted sexual exploration (i.e., sexual relations with casual partners/ friends or with sexual partners in one-night stands)" (Peter and Valkenburg 2008, 579). It is unlikely that the use of pornography can help marital relations seeing as the relationship values espoused in pornographic "story lines" often involve deceit, infidelity, promiscuity, disrespect, detachment, violence, coercion, and abuse.

The ripples of the negative effects of pornography extend far into our society. Once I did some outreach with a nongovernmental organization that dedicates to street mission with prostituted women. I asked them how is the situation of prostitution in Manila. They said "It is really increasing Father." When I enquired why, they replied "Pornography is the theory and prostitution is the practice." There is also a link between the use of adult pornography and subsequent transition to viewing of child pornography.[4] In the Philippines context, anecdotal reports exist linking sexual abuse of minors with pornography exposure. Sr Mary Pilar Verzosa RGS, reported that when sexually abused girls are asked to describe the abuser "many of them reveal that there is a proliferation of pornography in the house" and that the abuser "is addicted to cybersex or cell phone sex" (Verzosa 2011, 4).

From this comprehensive list of side effects one can easily see how dangerous online porn is. The body (usually of females or minors) is treated in a contemptible way as an object of pleasure and desire. The male body is also objectified in both heterosexual and gay porn. In my pastoral dialogues with men with same-sex attraction trying to live chastely, one of the main difficulties they have is the struggle to avoid watching gay pornography. When they do watch it, it inevitably leads to masturbation, with shame, discouragement, and often a relapse into unwanted same-sex behaviors. Users of gay porn also include women, and heterosexual men who may have hang ups about their own masculinity and are attracted by the athletic bodies of the actors. As the website of the US Conference of Catholic Bishops (n.d.) states, "Pornography is a grave offense against God and His gifts to men and women. God created men and women 'in His image' to share in His divine life. Rather than respecting and cherishing this image of God, pornography promotes a harmful and destructive anthropology (view of the human person). It teaches

Internet Pornography:
Some Medical and Spiritual Perspectives

people to use others as 'objects' - in this case, a means of selfish, lustful gratification."

Having presented clearly the deleterious personal, psychological, and social consequences of pornography use, we may ask why the medical establishment does not give a clearer denouncement of its harmfulness? In medical practice, it is important to refer the patient to the correct specialty such as cardiology for chest pain or dermatology for a skin rash. When it comes to evaluating the moral harm caused by pornography, the doctor can defer to the field of moral theology, the science which includes the moral appraisal of human behavior. Of course, a degree of intellectual humility is needed to recognize that medicine alone is unable to appreciate the wider dimensions of moral or spiritual harm caused by porn use to an individual. Failure to go beyond the limited scope of medicine can lead to "remarkable superficiality in the area of moral discernment" (Francis 2013, 62).

Many consumers of porn do not even consider they are doing anything wrong, as the conscience can become blinded by the habit of committing sin. A person with a lax or deformed conscience can be engaging in wrong, damaging themselves, and still feel fine, as Cardinal Ratzinger once underlined: "subjective conviction and the lack of doubts and scruples which follow there from do not justify man" (Ratzinger 1991, 1). Society, and medicine, can fall into a collective blunting of moral conscience with tragic consequences. Along with the Catholic Bishops of the

United States, we take seriously the insidious spread of the evil of pornography: "The pornography industry and its pervasive reach is a clear sign that pornography has become a structure of sin in our society" (US Conference of Catholic Bishops 2015, 10).

In the midst of such darkness, the rich and insightful perspective of Catholic teaching can indeed be a lamp for our feet and a light on our path (see Psalm 119:105). As Cardinal Newman (1875) put it eloquently in his 1875 letter to the Duke of Norfolk, with words that still ring true today:

> The sense of right and wrong ... , which is the first element in religion, is so delicate, so fitful, so easily puzzled, obscured, perverted, so subtle in its argumentative methods, so impressible by education, so biased by pride and passion, so unsteady in its flight, that, in the struggle for existence amid various exercises and triumphs of the human intellect, this sense is at once the highest of all teachers, yet the least luminous; and the Church, the Pope, the Hierarchy are, in the Divine purpose, the supply of an urgent demand. (Newman 1875, 78)

There is indeed an urgent demand for a deeper moral analysis of the issue according to the Catholic moral tradition. In the second part of this essay, we will look at the problem of pornography through various moral lenses (such as chastity, spirituality, sin, and prayer among others) in a bold effort to come to a more honest ethical appraisal. In doing so, conscious that the

Internet Pornography: Some Medical and Spiritual Perspectives

"truth will set us free" (John 8:32), we ask for the intervention of the Holy Spirit to help us rescue and rediscover the dignity and beauty of the body.

Part II: What Can Be Done?

A Call to Understand the Beauty of Chastity

For many in our contemporary world, "chastity" is a dirty word. It can be mistakenly be equated with being boring, prudish, and something only for dour priests and nuns. Actually, religious are called to be "celibate" (and joyful), but we are all called to be "chaste." A chaste person is able to harness the power of pure love in his or her heart. The Catholic vision of chastity far from being restrictive is actually liberating, as shown by a few excerpts from Church teaching:

- "Chastity includes an apprenticeship in self-mastery which is a training in human freedom. The alternative is clear: either man governs his passions and finds peace, or he lets himself be dominated by them and becomes unhappy" (Catechism of the Catholic Church 1997, n. 2339)
- "Chastity is the joyous affirmation of someone who knows how to live self-giving, free from any form of self-centered slavery. The chaste person is not self-centered, not involved in selfish relationships with other people. Chastity makes the personality harmonious. It matures it and fills it with inner peace" (Pontifical Council for the Family 1995, n. 17)

- Chastity is "spiritual energy capable of defending love from the perils of selfishness and aggressiveness" (John Paul II 1984, n. 33).

For me, these are beautiful definitions which reveal that the Catholic vision of chastity and sexuality is holistic, healthy, integrative, and life-giving. I will henceforth cite from some of the teachings of St. Alphonsus Liguori, our patron of moral theology in the Catholic church, whose writings on such topics are unparalleled in their depth, eloquence, and practical application. He does not underestimate the challenge to live chastely: "Great, then, is the excellence of chastity; but terrible indeed is the war that the flesh wages against men in order to rob them of that precious virtue. The flesh is the most powerful weapon that the devil employs in order to make us his slaves" (Liguori 1888, 247). But we are given the remedies: first, we must flee from all occasions of sin against purity. If we wish to conquer the sin of lust, we must take flight from danger to be victorious. As the book of Proverbs (6:27-28) reminds us "Can a man scoop fire into his lap without his clothes being burned? Can a man walk on hot coals without his feet being scorched?" Liguori also quotes Sirach 6:2 "Run away from sin like you would from a snake: If you go near it, it will bite you" and comments "We fly not only from the bite of a serpent, but also from contact with it and proximity to it" (Liguori 1888, 250).

Some mortification of the senses and the flesh is also suggested. "He who takes more wine than is necessary, shall certainly be molested with many carnal motions,

Internet Pornography:
Some Medical and Spiritual Perspectives

and shall scarcely be able to rule the flesh and make it obedient to the law of chastity" (Liguori 1888, 259). As for food, Liguori notes that "St. Thomas has written that when the devil is conquered by those whom he tempts to gluttony, he ceases to tempt them to impurity." (Liguori 1888, 260)

Prevention Is Better Than Cure

Ideally, better to never start looking at pornography in the first place. The prophet Jeremiah announced: "Death has come up through our windows, has entered our palaces" (Jeremiah 9:20). St Alphonsus Liguori commenting on this passage, wrote: "For as to defend a fortification it is not enough to lock the gates if the enemy be allowed to enter by the windows; so to preserve chastity all other means shall be unprofitable unless we carefully watch over the eyes" (Liguori 1888, 250-51). The eyes are the window to the heart. One seminarian approached Fr. Cantalamessa, the former Papal preacher, asking why it was wrong to gaze upon created beauty, especially beautiful women. After all, reasoned the seminarian, if God did not want us to enjoy such visual feasts why did he give us eyes? "It is true God gave us eyes," responded Fr. Cantalamessa, "but he also gave us eyelids to close them sometimes!"

For many, custody of the eyes may seem old-fashioned, but the enemy is real. The sexual images are stored in the brain, and the bad spirit, who prowls like a roaring lion (see 1 Peter 5:8), can conjure them up again at will. Pamela Paul, an American writer and current editor of the *New York Times* Book Review previously published a book in 2005 entitled *Pornified: How Pornography Is Transforming Our Lives, Our Relationships, and Our Families*. She wrote as part of her conclusion "passively accepting life in a pornified culture is helping pornography flourish, a fact which the industry is well aware. Our eyes become blinded by porn" (Paul 2005, 275).

What we look at can affect the way we think and see, after all "you are what you eat." At times, direct causality may be hard to ascertain, but facts such as after the release of the book *Fifty Shades of Grey*, there was an associated increase in sales of sex toys, as well as a greater interest in bondage, domination, submission, and masochism, should not escape our attention (Herbenick et al. 2020). It is worrisome that porn actors and producers themselves describe a greater emphasis on rough sex behaviors as a more recent trend in films produced. The content of pornography can influence the viewer, with recent behaviors mimicking those of what is called the "pornographic sexual script," so that sexual practices in life begin to mirror what is viewed on screen. Herbenick et al. in their comprehensive review of sexual practices among Americans who use pornography report that one-fifth of men and more than 11 percent of women had watched simulated rape (Herbenick et al., 2020). It does not require a randomized control trial to grasp how noxious and harmful such viewing could be. The same authors also note the worrying trend of choking and asphyxiation,

Internet Pornography: Some Medical and Spiritual Perspectives

with its concomitant dangers, appearing in the current repertoire of American sexual behavior, in a perverse kind of life imitating, not art, but pornography.

Importance of Prayer

In the fight against lust, we need the help of prayer, as "the spirit is willing but the flesh is weak" (Matthew 26:41). St. Paul already taught us "the one who sows for his flesh will reap corruption from the flesh, but the one who sows for the spirit will reap eternal life" (Galatians 6:8). The *Catechism of the Catholic Church* (1997) underlines this: "Prayer is a vital necessity. Proof from the contrary is no less convincing: if we do not allow the Spirit to lead us, we fall back into the slavery of sin" (n. 2744). Without prayer, we cannot live chastely. Saint Alphonsus Liguori acknowledged the great power of prayer to fight the temptations of the flesh:

> And it is especially to be remarked, that we cannot resist the impure temptations of the flesh, without recommending ourselves to God when we are tempted. This foe is so terrible that, when he fights with us, he, as it were, takes away all light; he makes us forget all our meditations, all our good resolutions; he also makes us also disregard the truths of faith, and even almost lose the fear of the divine punishments. For he conspires with our natural inclinations, which drive us with the greatest violence to the indulgence of sensual pleasures. Who in such a moment does not have recourse

> to God is lost. The only defense against this temptation is prayer. (Liguori 1992, 70-71)

And perhaps if I am not disturbed by this sin, by the grace of God, I can pray for the millions of those who are affected by it.

The believer who falls into the sin of pornography does well to be humble and seek recourse to the grace offered through the sacrament of reconciliation. Various researchers have tried to examine the attendant shame connected to pornography use. Some propose that the guilty feelings and shame arise from "moral incongruence" (i.e., feeling as if one's behaviors and values about those behaviors are misaligned) and that the act of viewing pornography goes against one's religious values rather than coming directly from the wrongful action of using pornography. For example, Perry and Whitehead conclude that "the connection between pornography use and sexual satisfaction, especially for men, depends largely on what viewing pornography means to consumers and their moral community and less so on the practice itself" (Perry and Whitehead 2019, 50). It seems to suggests that what is problematic is the religious belief not the pornography. I am reminded of the words of Pope Pius XII in 1946 who said "Perhaps the greatest sin in the world today is that men have begun to lose the sense of sin" (radio announcement). However, in another review article, Samuel L. Perry (quoted above), with Joshua B. Grubbs state clearly "Importantly, however, our findings do not imply that moral incongruence, perceived addiction to Internet

Internet Pornography:
Some Medical and Spiritual Perspectives

pornography, or general distress regarding pornography use should be arbitrarily dismissed as an artifact of religiously or morally based scruples around sexuality or pornography use" (Grubbs and Perry 2019, 34). These authors conclude that the distress experienced by a user of Internet pornography may arise from the dysfunction it causes in his or her life or also from the distress of behaving in a way that is morally incongruent, that is against his or her beliefs.

The concept of moral incongruence, whereby one feels distress when behavior is not in accord with purported values, sounds familiar to what St. Paul has expressed in his letter to the Romans: "For I know that good does not dwell in me, that is, in my flesh. The willing is ready at hand, but doing the good is not. For I do not do the good I want, but I do the evil I do not want. Now if I do what I do not want, it is no longer I who do it, but sin that dwells in me" (Romans 7:18-20). Thankfully, St. Paul later gives us the remedy to our moral incongruence: "Miserable one that I am! Who will deliver me from this mortal body? Thanks be to God through Jesus Christ our Lord" (Romans 7:24-25). If we don't live out what we believe, we will start to believe what we live. Prayer gives us the grace we need to live more coherent lives.

Time Well Spent

Many Saints, such as St Alphonsus Liguori, attest that we are easy sport for the devil when we are idle. Time is really a gift and should be valued, not wasted. Back in 2017, the Pornhub website claimed it transmitted more data every five minutes than the content of the New York Public library's 50 million books. No wonder many no longer have time to read books! I have met intelligent young men who ended up flunking college because they were spending most of their supposed study time looking at Internet pornography.

> Time is a treasure which can be found in this life alone; it is to be found neither in heaven nor in hell. In heaven there are no tears; but if the blessed could weep, this would be a cause for lamentation, that they had lost any time during this life in which they might have acquired greater glory for such time they now can never have. And you, my brother, how are you spending the time? (Liguori 1869, 78)

Fight the New Drug

There is a noble effort by a group called "Fight the New Drug" who describe themselves as "a nonreligious and nonlegislative organization that exists to provide individuals the opportunity to make an informed decision regarding pornography by raising awareness on its harmful effects using only science, facts, and personal accounts" (see their website and resources at https://fightthenewdrug.org/about/). A popular and effective slogan they use is "porn kills love," reminding us not to be naive.

Filters can be placed on Internet search engines to filter out explicit search results. Placing the laptop in a public place as well as having a person to whom one is

Internet Pornography:
Some Medical and Spiritual Perspectives

accountable to may be beneficial. Any existing pornographic material should be removed. After one formation on the ills of pornography, during the open forum, one brave soul grabbed the microphone to share his experience. The man described how he had actually managed to delete all the pornographic material from his laptop. I was very happy that the audience could hear such an encouraging testimony and decided to praise this man's courageous efforts. "Well done sir, it must have taken some will power to not watch the material but instead to delete it." "Oh," he said, "just to be clear, I actually watched it first then I deleted it all." I was a little stumped but tried to keep things in a positive vein, "Well, mmm, not quite what I recommend but it is still good to have deleted it, but of course even better not to watch it in the first place!"

Many people who struggle with the addiction to pornography are helped by forming or joining a support group.[5] Those struggling with the same problem can be of encouragement and give hope to those in need.[6]

Rediscovering the Dignity of the Body

Our body and our sexuality are an immense gift from God, the "giver of all good gifts" (see James 1:17). However, pornography tends to sully and cheapen the gift. Pope emeritus Benedict XVI in *Deus Caritas Est*, his very first encyclical, commented:

> the contemporary way of exalting the body is deceptive. Eros, reduced to pure "sex," has become a commodity, a mere "thing" to be bought and sold, or rather, man himself becomes a commodity which leads to a "a debasement of the human body: no longer is it integrated into our overall existential freedom; no longer is it a vital expression of our whole being, but it is more or less relegated to the purely biological sphere." (Benedict XVI 2005, n. 7)

The beauty of our bodies needs to be constantly and continually rediscovered. A renewed evangelization can help recapture the dignity of the body and counter the lie of pornography. Each person is sacred and possesses that immense dignity of being created in the image and likeness of God, in a doctrine known as the *imago Dei* (being made in the image of God). In God's great plan, the body is sacred. Pope John Paul II in his *Theology of the Body* stated that: "The body in fact, and only the body, is capable of making visible what is invisible: the spiritual and divine. It has been created to transfer into the visible reality of the world the mystery hidden from eternity in God, and thus to be a sign of it" (19:4) as well as underlining that "the person can never be considered a means to an end; above all never a means of pleasure" (John Paul II 1994, n. 12).

Pope Francis raised concerns in a recent congress on "Child Dignity in the Digital World." He said that

Internet Pornography:
Some Medical and Spiritual Perspectives

> the dramatic growth of pornography in the digital world is, in itself, most serious, the fruit of a general loss of the sense of human dignity ... The safe and sound growth of our young is a noble goal worth pursuing; it has far greater value than mere economic profit gained at the risk of harming young people (Francis 2019).

We as Catholic healthcare professionals can help counter the commodification and objectification of the person through pornography by making a personal and collective effort to promote the dignity of the body, the beauty of sexuality and the gift of each person. The crux of renewed evangelization is to see the other as beautiful, not as an object of desire, but as a subject, made in the image and likeness of God. This evangelization necessarily includes the digital world, so that, as Pope emeritus Benedict XVI encouraged us, "in the world of the internet, which enables billions of images to appear on millions of screens throughout the world, the face of Christ needs to be seen and his voice heard" (Benedict XVI 2010, n. 113).

Notes

1. Care needs to be taken even when reading reports of data about pornography use as a certain sexual curiosity can be aroused.

2. This young man's experience supports what is known as the "picture superiority effect" whereby pornographic images seem to have an indelible type of

imprinting in the cortex (Owens et al. 2012, 114). Interestingly, "many men claim that when they view an erotic image it gets 'burned into their brains'." The chemical responsible for this is norepinephrine, which is also referred to as the "snapshot chemical" (Kleponis 2019, 44).

3. For a helpful and detailed review of the proposed neuroscientific basis underlying addiction to Internet pornography, see "Neuroscience of Internet Pornography Addiction: A Review and Update" by Love et al. (2015). This review presents strong neuroscientific evidence for the potentially addictive nature of Internet pornography and critiques somewhat the American Psychiatric Association for its "misunderstanding of addiction neuroscience" in drawing attention to Internet gaming, yet not to internet pornography "despite substantial overlap in activation of the reward system of the brain, and despite the potential for the exhibition of similar psychosocial behaviors and psychosocial consequences" (Love et al. 2015, 413).

4. The International Justice Mission (IJM) is now making intensive efforts to stop the proliferation and spread of online sexual exploitation of children (OSEC), "particularly the use of a child to make sexually explicit photos, videos, or live shows on the internet in exchange for money." International Justice Mission. 2019. "OSEC destroys families." IJMPH Fact sheet March.

5. The "Integrity Restored" website is a most helpful online resource, providing education and pastoral resources for those affected by pornography (https://integrityrestored.com/).

6. For a helpful account, in question-and-answer style, of the dangers of pornography and how to overcome an addiction to pornography see, Evert (2013).

References

American Psychiatric Association. 2013. *Diagnostic and Statistical Manual of Mental Disorders.* 5th ed. Arlington, VA: American Psychiatric Publishing.

Baranowski, Andreas M., Romina Vogl, and Rudolf Stark. 2019. "Prevalence and Determinants of Problematic Online Pornography Use in a Sample of German Women" *The Journal of Sexual Medicine* 16, n. 8: 1274-82.

Benedict, Pope. 2005. *Deus Caritas Est.*

Benedict, Pope. 2010. *Verbum Domini.*

Catechism of the Catholic Church. 1997. 2nd ed. Vatican City: Libreria Editrice Vaticana.

Catholic Bishops' Conference of the Philippines. 2016. "Created for Love, Created for Chastity." *A Pastoral Response to the Grave Evil of Pornography*, February 10.

de Alarcón, Rube´n, Javier I. de la Iglesia, Nerea M. Casado, and Angel L. Montejo. 2019. "Online Porn

Addiction: What We Know and What We Don't - A Systematic Review." *Journal of Clinical Medicine* 15, n. 8: 1-20.

Dwulit, Aleksandra Diana, and Piotr Rzymski. 2019. "The Potential Associations of Pornography Use with Sexual Dysfunctions: An Integrative Literature Review of Observational Studies." *Journal of Clinical Medicine* 8, no.7: pii: E914.

Eberstadt, Mary, and Mary Anne Layden. 2010. *The Social Costs of Pornography: A Statement of Findings and Recommendations.* Princeton, NJ: The Witherspoon Institute.

Evert, Jason (Eds). 2013. *If You Really Loved Me.* Denver, CO: Totus Tuus Press, 117-30.

Fagan, Patrick F. 2009. "The Effects of Pornography on Individuals, Marriage, Family and Community." *Research Synthesis from the Family Research Council*, Washington, DC, December.

Fisher, William A., and Taylor Kohut. 2017. "Pornography Viewing: Keep Calm and Carry On." *The Journal of Sexual Medicine* 14, n. 3: 320-22.

Francis, Pope. 2013. *Evangelii Gaudium.*

Francis, Pope. 2019. "Child Dignity in the Digital World." 14 November.

Grubbs, Joshua B., and Samuel L. Perry. 2019. "Moral Incongruence and Pornography Use: A Critical Review and Integration." *The Journal of Sex Research* 56, n. 1: 29-37.

Internet Pornography:
Some Medical and Spiritual Perspectives

Herbenick, Debby, Tsung-Chieh Fu, Paul Wright, Bryant Paul, Ronna Gradus, Jill Bauer, and Rashida Jones. 2020. "Diverse Sexual Behaviors and Pornography Use: Findings from a Nationally Representative Probability Survey of Americans Aged 18 to 60 Years." *The Journal of Sexual Medicine* 17, n. 4: 623-633.

John Paul II, Pope. 1984. *Familiaris Consortio.*

John Paul II, Pope. 1994. Letter to Families (*Gratissimam Sane*).

John Paul II, Pope. 2006. *Man and Woman He Created Them: A Theology of the Body.* Translated by Michael Waldstein. Boston, MA: Pauline Books and Media.

Kleponis, Peter. 2019. *Integrity Restored: Helping Catholic Families Win the Battle against Pornography*, Revised and Expanded ed. Ohio: Emmaus Road Publishing.

Liguori, Alphonsus. 1869. *Preparation for Death.* Revised editing by Orby Shipley. Philadelphia: J. B. Lippincott.

Liguori, Alphonsus. 1888. *Discourse on the Necessity of Mental Prayer for Priests, in Dignity and Duties of the Priest, or Selva.* Edited by Eugene Grimm. New York: Elias Frederick Schauer.

Liguori, Alphonsus. 1992. *Oppitz, Joseph. Alphonsus Liguori - The Redeeming Love of Christ.* New York: New City Press.

Love, Todd, Christian Laier, Matthias Brand, Linda Hatch, and Raju Hajela. 2015. "Neuroscience of Internet Pornography Addiction: A Review and Update." *Behavioral Sciences* 5:388-433.

Newman, John Henry. 1875. *A Letter Addressed to his Grace, the Duke of Norfolk, on Occasion of Mr. Gladstone's Recent Expostulation*. New York: The Catholic Publication Society.

Owens, Eric W., Richard J. Behun, Jill C. Manning, and Rory C. Reid. 2012. "The Impact of Internet Pornography on Adolescents: A Review of the Research." *Sexual Addiction & Compulsivity* 19:1-2, 99-122.

Paul, Pamela. 2005. *Pornified: How Pornography Is Transforming Our Lives, Our Relationships, and Our Families*. New York: Henry Holt and Company.

Perry, Samuel L., and Andrew L. Whitehead. 2019. "Only Bad for Believers? Religion, Pornography Use, and Sexual Satisfaction Among American Men." *The Journal of Sex Research* 56, no.1: 50-61.

Peter, Jochen, and Patti M. Valkenburg. 2008. "Adolescents' Exposure to Sexually Explicit Internet Material, Sexual Uncertainty, and Attitudes toward Uncommitted Sexual Exploration: Is There a Link?" *Communication Research* 35, no. 5: 579-601.

Peter, Jochen, and Patti M. Valkenburg. 2016. "Adolescents and Pornography: A Review of 20 Years of Research." *The Journal of Sex Research* 54, n. 2: 509-31.

Pius XII, Pope. 1946. "Radio Message of His Holiness Pius XII to the Participants in the National Catechetical Congress of the United States in Boston." Pontifical Palace in Castel Gandolfo, Italy. Saturday, 26 October.

Pontifical Council for the Family. 1995. *The Truth and Meaning of Human Sexuality: Guidelines for Education Within the Family.*

Pornhub. 2019. "The 2019 Year in Review." 11 December.

Ratzinger, Joseph. 1991. "Conscience and Truth." Presented at the 10th Workshop for Bishops, February 1991 Dallas, TX, USA.

Rissel, Chris, Juliet Richters, Richard O. de Visser, Alan McKee, Anna Yeung, and Theresa Caruana. 2016. "A Profile of Pornography Users in Australia: Findings from the Second Australian Study of Health and Relationships." *The Journal of Sex Research* 54, n. 2: 227-40.

Sniewski, Luke, Panteá Farvida, and Phil Carter. 2018. "The Assessment and Treatment of Adult Heterosexual Men with Self-perceived Problematic Pornography Use: A Review." *Addictive Behaviors* 77:217-24.

US Conference of Catholic Bishops. n.d. "Pornography."

US Conference of Catholic Bishops. 2015. "Create in Me a Clean Heart." A Pastoral Response to Pornography.

Vatican Council II. 1965. *Gaudium et Spes.*

Verzosa, Mary Pilar R. G. S. 2011. "Pornography, Rape and Incest." In *CBCP Monitor* 15, n. 15: July 18-31, A4.

Villena, Alejandro, Maria Contreras, and Carlos Chiclana. 2017. "Consequences of Pornography Use." *The Journal of Sexual Medicine* 14, n. 5: e254.

Webroot. n.d. "Internet Pornography by the Numbers; A Significant Threat to Society."

DEVASTATING CONSEQUENCES OF SEX TRAFFICKING ON WOMEN'S HEALTH

Summary

Sex trafficking has devastating consequences on the physical and mental well-being of millions of women around the world. These trafficking victims often come in contact with medical personnel, and these encounters with suitably prepared staff can be a step toward healing of the victims. The Catholic Church, especially through Pope Francis, is making strenuous efforts to help curb the spread of sex trafficking.

On the first of November, I celebrated the Holy Mass of All the Saints at a center for rehabilitation of female survivors of sex trafficking. They are being taken care of by Religious Sisters who have a specific dedication in this area.[1] The Sister in charge commented to me that same-sex attraction (SSA) was commonly observed among such girls, including sexualized behavior with the same sex. I was asked how we should consider this phenomenon of SSA in this context and how best to help these young victims. The experience of visiting the shelter made me reflect on the health consequences - physical, mental, and spiritual - of the traumatic experience these girls have been through.

I would like to answer this pastoral question of female SSA, post-sex trafficking by first looking at the broader picture of human trafficking for sexual purposes and briefly showing its devastating impact on women's health globally. Next, I will share some specific points of Catholic moral teaching on prostitution and human trafficking before considering the specific role of healthcare workers in identifying and assisting victims of trafficking. The Religious Sisters' general approach in ministering to the victims of sex trafficking and prostitution will then be outlined, before closing with some pastoral considerations regarding the experience of SSA in this specific context.

Human Trafficking

In 2017, Archbishop Bernardito Auza delivered a lecture titled "The Holy See and the Fight Against Human Trafficking" (Auza 2017). He estimated that thirty-six million people were trafficked in 2016. Archbishop Auza stated that:

> according to the 2016 Global Report on Trafficking in Persons released two months ago by the UN Office on Drugs and Crime, human trafficking is a 32 billion dollar industry, running third behind arms and drug trafficking. Fifty- one percent of the victims are women, 21 percent are men, 20 percent girls and 8 percent boys. (Auza 2017)

For women victims of trafficking, 72 percent of them are trafficked for sexual exploitation. This would mean that globally approximately 13 million women are sex trafficked annually.

Devastating Consequences of Sex Trafficking on Women's Health

The "Trafficking in Persons Report" (TIP report) released by the U.S. Department of State explains "'Trafficking in persons' and 'human trafficking' have been used as umbrella terms for the act of recruiting, harboring, transporting, providing, or obtaining a person for compelled labor or commercial sex acts through the use of force, fraud, or coercion" (U.S. Department of State 2016, 30). Trafficking can be for various purposes such as forced labor and organ retrieval, but by far the majority of victims are trafficked for sexual purposes. The same TIP report defines sex trafficking in the following way:

> When an adult engages in a commercial sex act, such as prostitution, as the result of force, threats of force, fraud, coercion or any combination of such means, that person is a victim of trafficking. Under such circumstances, perpetrators involved in recruiting, harboring, enticing, transporting, providing, obtaining, patronizing, soliciting, or maintaining a person for that purpose are guilty of sex trafficking of an adult. Sex trafficking also may occur within debt bondage, as individuals are compelled to continue in prostitution through the use of unlawful "debt," purportedly incurred through their transportation, recruitment, or even their "sale" - which exploiters insist they must pay off before they can be free. An adult's initial consent to participate in prostitution is not legally determinative: if one is thereafter held in service through psychological manipulation or

physical force, he or she is a trafficking victim and should receive benefits outlined in the Palermo Protocol and applicable domestic laws. (U.S. Department of State 2016, 30)

Health Consequences[2]

In the work of Lederer and Wetzel, one victim noted the following:

> During that time I saw 10 to 20 men a day. I did what he said because he got violent when I sassed him. I took all kinds of drugs - even though I didn't really like most of them. Over the years I had pimps and customers who hit me, punched me, kicked me, beat me, slashed me with a razor. I had forced unprotected sex and got pregnant three times and had two abortions at [a clinic]. Afterward, I was back out on the street again. I have so many scars all over my body and so many injuries and so many illnesses. I have hepatitis C and stomach and back pain and a lot of psychological issues. I tried to commit suicide several times. (Lederer and Wetzel 2014, 61)

Most female victims of sex trafficking end up in forced prostitution and/or the pornography industry. Melissa Farley states that "throughout history, regardless of its legal status, prostitution has had a devastating impact on women's health" (Farley 2004, 1097). This can be seen in the many physical and psychological consequences of this destructive lifestyle. Some findings include the following:

Devastating Consequences of Sex Trafficking on Women's Health

- Sexual violence and physical assault are the norm for women in all types of prostitution.

- Health problems include exhaustion, frequent viral illness, STDs, vaginal infections, back aches, sleeplessness, depression, headaches, stomach aches, and eating disorders.

- Post-traumatic stress disorder is a consequence of prostitution as are mood disorders such as dissociation and depression.

- Prostituted women are at a higher risk of being murdered. (Farley 2004, 1087-125)

Drug and alcohol abuse is a common finding among prostituted women. In most it serves as a mechanism to partially numb the horror and misery they experience.

The handbook Caring for Trafficked Persons: Guidance for Health Providers reports that "as is the case with victims of torture, individuals who have been trafficked are likely to sustain multiple physical or psychological injuries and illnesses and report a complex set of symptoms (IOM et al. 2009, 17). Where the victim is a minor (younger than 18 years of age) the TIP report notes that "Sex trafficking has devastating consequences for children, including long-lasting physical and psychological trauma, disease (including HIV/AIDS), drug addiction, unwanted pregnancy, malnutrition, social ostracism, and even death" (U.S. Department of State 2016, 30).

Classification

Various classifications have been used to enumerate the wide spectrum of health consequences of prostitution and sex trafficking. Lederer and Wetzel report the following categories: physical health symptoms; psychological symptoms; reproductive issues; violence, abuse, and humiliation; and substance abuse (Lederer and Wetzel 2014). Willis and Levy list the following:[3] infectious disease, pregnancy, mental illness, substance abuse, violence and malnutrition (Willis and Levy 2002). No attempt will be made here to produce a definitive review of the myriad health consequences of sex trafficking. The point is rather to show the complexity and vast range of deleterious effects of trafficking for sexual purposes on the affected individual.[4] It is also of note that same-sex attraction post-trafficking is not mentioned.

To fully consider the negative impact of sex trafficking on women, we should not overlook the consequences in the wives, partners, or girlfriends of the men who buy the bodies of trafficked women. The sin of the male has far-reaching consequences in all his relationships with significant other women in his life. Not only will he place his, let us say, wife at some medical risk (consider the risk of infection from HIV, for example), but morally he will be failing to give his wife the purity and quality of love that he promised through the sacrament of marriage.

Let us now look at some aspects of Catholic Church teaching.

Devastating Consequences of Sex Trafficking on Women's Health

Selected Elements of Catholic Moral Teaching on Prostitution and Human Trafficking

Biblical

Rahab was a woman in the Old Testament who was known to be a prostitute. However, she was open to God's will and was saved because of her faithful help to Israel (see Jo 2:1ff and 6:17ff). The New Testament writers acknowledge both her faith (Heb 11:40) and good works (Jas 2:25). She is also mentioned in the family tree of Jesus (Mt 1:5).

In the New Testament, we know that Jesus himself was not ashamed to associate with women of ill repute and frequently stepped in to defend and save them (see Lk 7:36-50 and Jn 8:1-11). Jesus even provoked the chief priests and the elders of the people by announcing, "Amen, I say to you, tax collectors and prostitutes are entering the kingdom of God before you" (Mt 21:31).

Lives of the Saints

Various holy men and women did pastoral work to ease the suffering of prostituted women and attempted to form the conscience of society about the wrongs of buying the body of another. Some specific examples may enlighten us. Blessed Gennaro Maria Sarnelli, an Italian Redemptorist (1702-44), dedicated himself to stopping the spread of prostitution in Naples, Italy. Saint Alphonsus Liguori, founder of the Redemptorists, and the patron saint of moral theology in the Catholic Church, wrote a commentary on the concern of Gennaro for women caught up in this predicament:

In Naples, his zeal on behalf of the prostitutes was well known; everyone spoke about how much he worked on their behalf. To free them from their shameful life, he collected alms and preached on this evil in order to lessen the number of prostitutes. Every feast day he would preach in the busy square opposite the Church of S. Matteo for this purpose. He also persuaded the archbishop's confraternity to engage in a retreat on this topic. As for himself, he held back nothing of his own, even to the point of exhaustion, to help these poor women caught in this sinful life or those in danger of falling into it. He helped many of them escape from it at his own expense. He looked everywhere there might be a chance he would find one of these pitiful women and free her. There were two for whom he gave special help for more than two years; he relocated them and provided them a place to live and even bought furniture for them.

Besides these, there were many others for whom he found places to live. It was for this work that he sought donations in many homes, not only in religious places, but also at some houses where he was so unwelcome that he once said he felt like he would die. In all this, he suffered insults, doors slammed in his face, and the typical risks that come with asking for alms. He also suffered a great deal of persecution and personal injury. (Chiovaro 2003, 60-61)

St. Alphonsus spoke further of the danger Gennaro exposed himself to in this mission:

> This work caused our Don Gennaro to often live in mortal danger, liable to being killed by the pimps of these poor women. Because of the danger, his parents kept trying to stop him out of fear of what might befall him, and perhaps the whole family. Nevertheless, he protested that he was ready to suffer any consequence and, in fact, would consider it his good fortune if, for a work that gives such glory to God, he even had to lose his life! (Chiovaro 2003, 61)

Blessed Gennaro Maria Sarnelli died worn out from his labors at 41 years of age. On his tombstone part of his epitaph reads "Repressed the scourge of prostitution."

Another saintly example of care for victims of prostitution is St. Maria Micaela Desmaisieres. She was born to Spanish nobility in 1809. Her father was a high-ranking officer in the Spanish Army and her mother was lady-in-waiting of the then Spanish Queen, Maria Luisa de Parma. St. Maria Micaela founded the congregation known as the "Sisters Adorers," now present in around twenty- three countries, who dedicate their lives to Eucharistic adoration and to ministering to women victims of prostitution and sex trafficking.

Magisterium

In 1948, Pope Pius XII stated that

> The most formidable obstacle to your action [against prostitution] is neither the declared hostility of the enemies of God and souls, nor that of the libertines, nor traffickers in the white slave trade who shamelessly enrich themselves. This hostility is completely understandable.... What is odd is that it is necessary to vanquish the careless, ironic, even indifferent Christians who believe themselves to be upright, convinced and practicing Catholics. (Rey-Mermet 1998, 120-21)

In *Gaudium et Spes* we find

> whatever is opposed to life itself, such as ... prostitution, the selling of women and children ... are infamies indeed. They poison human society, and they do more harm to those who practice them than to those who suffer from the injury. Moreover, they are a supreme dishonor to the Creator. (Vatican Council II 1965, n. 27)

The *Catechism* declares

> Prostitution does injury to the dignity of the person who engages in it, reducing the person to an instrument of sexual pleasure. The one who pays sins gravely against himself: he violates the chastity to which his Baptism pledged him and defiles his body, the temple of the Holy Spirit. (Catechism 1997, n. 2355)

Pope Francis[5]

Archbishop Auza tells us:

Devastating Consequences of Sex Trafficking on Women's Health

Cardinal Jorge Bergoglio had already been exposed to human trafficking in Buenos Aires, where he was archbishop for fifteen years prior to his papal election. In a daily homily, after noting that Jesus "stands with our brothers and sisters who live under slavery," he commented, "We have been taught that slavery has been abolished, but you know what? It's not true, because in the city of Buenos Aires slavery is not abolished. In this city slavery is present in different forms." Soon after his election, he sent a hand-written note to his fellow Argentine, Bishop Marcelo Sanchez Sorondo, Chancellor of the Pontifical Academy of Sciences and the Pontifical Academy for Social Sciences, in which he wrote, "I believe it would be good to examine human trafficking and modern slavery. Organ trafficking could be examined in connection with human trafficking. Many thanks, Francis." (Auza 2017)

Our current pope has been very pro-active in his advocacy to denounce sex trafficking. He has given numerous addresses and organized various conferences to examine the problem of human trafficking and to look for possible solutions to try to reduce the incidence of modern-day slavery. In *Evangelii Gaudium*, his apostolic exhortation on the proclamation of the Gospel in today's world, he devotes a whole paragraph to the theme:

> I have always been distressed at the lot of those who are victims of various kinds of human

trafficking. How I wish that all of us would hear God's cry: "Where is your brother?" (Gen 4:9). Where is your brother or sister who is enslaved? Where is the brother and sister whom you are killing each day in clandestine warehouses, in rings of prostitution, in children used for begging, in exploiting undocumented labor. Let us not look the other way. There is greater complicity than we think. The issue involves everyone! This infamous network of crime is now well established in our cities, and many people have blood on their hands as a result of their comfortable and silent complicity. (Francis 2013a, n. 211)

In an Easter Sunday address, Pope Francis said,

Peace in the whole world, still divided by greed looking for easy gain, wounded by the selfishness which threatens human life and the family, selfishness that continues in human trafficking, the most extensive form of slavery in this twenty-first century; human trafficking is the most extensive form of slavery in this twenty-first century! (Francis 2013b)

More recently the pope addressed the participants of Religious in Europe Net- working Against Trafficking and Exploitation (RENATE). The group was in Rome for their 2nd European Assembly with the theme "Ending Trafficking Begins with Us." The pontiff, talking about wounds in the world, said

Devastating Consequences of Sex Trafficking on Women's Health

> One of the most troubling of those open wounds is the trade in human beings, a modern form of slavery, which violates the God-given dignity of so many of our brothers and sisters and constitutes a true crime against humanity. While much has been accomplished in acknowledging its gravity and extent, much more needs to be done on the level of raising public consciousness and effecting a better coordination of efforts by governments, the judiciary, law-enforcement officials and social workers. (Francis 2016)

Having briefly outlined some pertinent aspects of Catholic moral teaching on prostitution and sex trafficking, we now consider the role of healthcare workers in assisting victims of trafficking.

Specific Role of Healthcare Professionals

In one study, 88 percent of trafficking victims reported accessing healthcare facilities during their experience of being trafficked and, of these, 63 percent were seen at an emergency department (Lederer and Wetzel 2014, 77). In the initial interview some red flags that may indicate a situation of trafficking are:

- Someone else is speaking for the patient

- Patient is not aware of his or her location, the current date, or time

JESUS THE DIVINE PHYSICIAN

- Patient exhibits fear, anxiety, PTSD, submission, or tension
- Patient shows signs of physical or sexual abuse, medical neglect, or torture
- Patient is reluctant to explain his or her injury
- Patient reports an unusually high numbers of sexual partners
- Patient does not have appropriate clothing for the weather or venue
- Patient uses language common in the commercial sex industry
- Patient is under the age of 18 and is involved in the commercial sex industry
- Tattoos may be present (or other forms of branding that say "For sale," "Property of ...,") (National Human Trafficking Resource Center 2016, 1)

Additional helpful reminders for healthcare staff are given in the handbook *Caring for Trafficked Persons: Guidelines for Health Providers*:

1. To consider each consultation as an opportunity for improving the health of the trafficked person.

2. The safety of trafficked persons, self and staff is paramount.

Devastating Consequences of Sex Trafficking on Women's Health

3. Provide good care and avoid discrimination. Any prejudice or disdain on the part of the healthcare worker should not interfere with good care.

4. Be prepared with referral information and contact details for trusted support persons. It is helpful if healthcare workers are familiar with the protocol in their hospital of what to do if they suspect that the patient is a victim of trafficking.

5. Knowing the vast range of negative health consequences of sex trafficking necessitates the performance of a comprehensive health assessment. (IOM et al. 2009, 27-29)

Additional questions may be appropriate:

• *Head/eyes/ears/nose/throat*: Any history of head trauma? Examine the skull for bruises, depressions or healed lacerations. Frequent headaches? Any pharyngeal trauma (lacerations, tears)?

• *Neck*: Any history of strangulation?

• *Cardiovascular*: Any trauma to the chest?

• *Respiratory*: Possible exposure to TB? (Living conditions? Number of people sharing one bedroom? Ventilation?)

• *Gastrointestinal*: Abdominal trauma?

• *Genitourinary*: Forced sex, or sexual trauma that includes foreign objects? Enuresis or encopresis (a potential result of sexual abuse)?

- *Musculoskeletal*: Repetitive and non-repetitive work-related injuries? Fractures? History of physical abuse such as burns? Contractures?

- *Neurological/behavioral*: Seizure activity (may also need to consider pseudo-seizures)? Sleep disorders (inability to fall asleep, frequent awakenings, nightmares)? Any history of head trauma?

- *Nutrition*: Any nutritional deficiencies (food intake, content)? Disordered eating (e.g., anorexia or bulimic behavior)?

- *Dermatological*: Burns (e.g., cigarette burns, scalds from hot water)?

Areas of specific concern include mental health and sexual and reproductive health. A thorough evaluation and work up of these areas is often indicated. Where medical evidence will be used in possible assault/rape cases or for criminal proceedings against traffickers, a specialized forensic exam may be needed and should be conducted by suitably trained persons.[6]

It may be useful for healthcare personnel to receive suitable training to identify victims of sex trafficking, and how to treat them, at the beginning of their professional training, not just when they are in the field.[7]

Trauma In Carers

The negative effects of sex trafficking may extend to the healthcare staff caring for the victims. This vicarious

Devastating Consequences of Sex Trafficking on Women's Health

trauma (also known as compassion fatigue or secondary traumatic stress):

> refers to the negative reactions that can occur when professionals repeatedly witness or hear about victims' difficult experiences of trauma, violence, and abuse. The signs of vicarious trauma resemble post-traumatic stress disorder, and can include emotional, behavioral, and physical symptoms, such as anxiety, depression, disturbed sleep, change in appetite, irritability, nightmares, loss of empathy, and numbness. (U.S. Department of State 2016, 38)

IOM et al. report that "it is not unusual for people working with trafficked persons to experience emotions of anger, pain, frustration, sadness, shock, horror and distress. The work could also affect energy levels and cause disturbed sleep, somatic complaints and hyper-arousal" (IOM et al. 2009, 97).

Having considered some salient features of the role of healthcare workers in identifying and treating victims of sex trafficking, we now turn to an in-depth description of the Sisters' general approach in ministering to the victims of sex trafficking and prostitution.

Ministry To Victims Of Sex Trafficking And Prostitution[8]

The information in the following sections, presented in question-and-answer style, was obtained in an interview with one of the Sisters involved in the ministry.

- *How are the victims of sex trafficking and prostitution identified?*

The young women can be referred by governmental agencies, such as the Department of Social Welfare and Development, or non-governmental agencies, such as the International Justice Mission. They can also be referred through the "drop in" center (see the "Drop in" welcome house section).

- *How are they housed?*

The young women are housed in one of three separate facilities: the "drop in" center (a form of temporary shelter), the "recovery" (rehabilitation) center, and the "after-care" center, depending on their needs and stages of recovery.

"Drop in" welcome house[9]

The welcome house has open doors so the women can come and go as they please. They are not bound to reside here but can rest, eat, and stay overnight for as long as they want. Help is given including: support groups for sharing, counselling, and recollections. Assistance is offered to help them find other job opportunities. Medical examinations are also available.

Recovery center

The recovery center offers the young women a live-in experience from six months up to one year for the first stage of intensive processing involving counselling, psycho-spiritual inner journeying, and physical processing to assist in release of pent-up negative emotions such as anger. The spiritual aspects of healing are described in more detail in the following paragraphs.

Medical examinations are carried out.

Following the period of personal healing, attempts are then made to try to reconnect the young women with their family. The family need to be vetted as there are cases when they are the ones asking the young woman to return to prostitution as a source of the family livelihood.

Assistance is given when needed to help the young women prepare to give testimonies in court against trafficking rings.

Later in their recovery process they can have classes in a home-schooling context. They may also be given leadership roles in the center to assist in the care of the newly admitted girls even becoming a role model for them. In executing their responsibilities, the leaders can also be assessed [to see] if they [are] ready to pass to the next stage called after care.

After-care center

From the recovery center the young women can pass to the after-care center. This focuses on the transition stage, helping them reintegrate into society. The schedule is less structured and emphasis is given to help the young women constructively plan their future:

such as taking on other work or going to study in college. They are also monitored when they return to their family or community. Continuous formation is also offered.

- ***What is the Sisters' approach to healing these patients?***

The general approach is holistic and considers the following dimensions: physical, psychological, and spiritual. The process of possible recovery is patient and gradual, recognizing that there should be a process of healing and that it takes time (often years). The approach is also hopeful, knowing that although the healing process can be involved, demanding, and challenging, for the women and those helping, the ideal goal is the full reintegration into society. The relationship with the family of origin is also taken into consideration.

- ***Is there a role for prayer/spirituality?***

Yes, a very important role! Spiritual sessions are an essential part of the recovery process and include prayer, sharing, Mass and recollections. The sacrament of reconciliation is also offered. These young women, many of whom are deeply wounded, can only be healed with the assistance of God's grace.

Many of them also come to the center not really knowing Christ. They know of him, from a religious upbringing, but what really helps them is to know him in a more personal way: to experience his love in their brokenness and woundedness. Once they develop a relationship with the Creator and start to see something good about themselves, the healing can more easily occur.

- *Are there specific interventions/situations to be avoided?*

The recovery process has to be integral and holistic. The spiritual recovery needs to be integrated with solid human formation and psychological support. The spiritual and human need to heal hand-in-hand. A danger to be avoided is a rehabilitation that would be "excessively" spiritual, and not taking into full consideration the complexity of the woundedness of the person. The wounds do not only affect the spirit of the person! The women also need to be in touch with their human feelings and brokenness to ensure an eventual holistic recovery process.

- *Are there any generalizable observations?*

There are three that can be mentioned here. The first is that the centers need to create an atmosphere where the young women feel loved, accepted and not judged for what has happened to them. The second is to note the great challenge in assisting the women in acquiring a new set of gospel-inspired values. Often certain wrong values have become "normal." For example, many do not know the wrongness of abortion. Their values have often become distorted. Another example is that they may have been led to believe that the incestuous abuse they incurred in their family of origin, prior to the experience of being prostituted, was just a form of "playing." This work of trying to evangelize their pre-conceived values is very challenging as some wrong values seem to be deeply ingrained. Finally, it is not uncommon for a woman to abandon the recovery process and to return to that former way of life. Sometimes they have to again hit "rock bottom" and surrender to the Lord again before returning once more to rehabilitation. It is an experience similar to that of the prodigal son who lost everything before "coming to his senses" and deciding to return to the Father (see Lk 15:17). Those caring have to be full of patience, not scandalized by human fragility, and always ready to offer the healing remedy of God's mercy.

- *Any predictors of successful outcomes?*

Two key predictors are openness and family support. The openness of the young woman is an essential feature of the recovery process. The more open they are to the intervention process the more likely they will make a wholesome recovery.

A solid family foundation also helps in the recovery process. Sometimes the family was previously intact but a traumatic life event eventually led to the young woman being prostituted. During recovery, if they had at least some experience of being loved in a family environment beforehand, it greatly assists the healing process.

- *Any predictors of poor outcomes?*

Well, really, the opposite to those previously mentioned. If the young woman is closed, it is not easy for the assistance or healing grace to enter deeply into the heart and life of the wounded woman. The woman needs to be able to open up about her experiences. And if the woman has no experience of love in the family, it makes recovery more difficult, as does having no current loving family to return to for support. Finally, co-existing personality disorders may complicate the healing process.

We now return to the pastoral issue of SSA in these young women.

Same-sex Attraction in Females Post-Sex Trafficking[10]

In the rehabilitation center (mentioned in the Introduction section), it is observed that SSA is common in women who have been victims of sex trafficking. To pastorally assist such young women, it is helpful to establish a baseline of whether they had same-sex feelings or experiences prior to their trafficking experience.

Some of the girls actually did have SSA prior to trafficking. They explained that their same-sex feelings seemed to originate following their experience of childhood abuse at the hands of males. It is well known that such abuse may contribute to the development of later SSA (McTavish 2014b, 3-4). Following abuse, anti-male sentiments may develop, including fear, mistrust, and a general feeling of being unsafe around males. One girl shared that she initially had an interest in boys, but this disappeared after her experience of abuse, such that later she became more confident sharing only with other girls. All these anti-male feelings were compounded when these girls subsequently became victims of sex trafficking. Abuse alone produces a deep woundedness in the psyche of a young person, and how much more profound will the woundedness be after the experience of being trafficked. Deep wounds are not healed overnight, and the recovery process is usually long and complex.

Some girls, with or without a previous history of abuse, were known to have developed same-sex feelings only *after* the experience of being trafficked. On reviewing the general literature surrounding sex trafficking, this author can find no mention of SSA in females post-exposure to sex trafficking. The comprehensive and highly influential "Global report on Trafficking in Persons" produced annually by the UN Office on Drugs and Crime does not make any reference to this phenomenon, although the group of persons who are LGBT is mentioned various times and is singled out for special concern.[11]

Same-sex feelings developing post- trafficking could be partly explained by the process outlined above where the woman loses trust and confidence with males and feels safer depositing her feelings and heart in the arms of another female. In such cases the SSA could be transient or passing as the trauma heals. Often young females may have passing attractions or "crushes" on other girls. The late John Harvey, founder of Courage, the Roman Catholic ministry for persons with SSA, advised

Devastating Consequences of Sex Trafficking on Women's Health

> The adolescent girl often confuses a "crush" she has on an older girl or a female teacher as a form of homosexuality. She should be shown that she is simply going through a stage of strong admiration and needs to take care not to make an idol out of another person. Meanwhile, she must continue to seek friends within her peer group and learn to form good human relationships with both sexes. (Harvey 2007, 34-35)

Such girls in rehabilitation, experiencing same-sex feelings after being trafficked, may be seeking to fulfill legitimate needs for affection and attention from other females, but need to learn how to do so in healthy, non-erotic ways. In a word, they need to "relearn" the virtue of chastity. The *Catechism* defines chastity as "the successful integration of sexuality within the person and thus the inner unity of man in his bodily and spiritual being ... The virtue of chastity therefore involves the integrity of the person and the integrality of the gift" (Catechism 1997, n. 2337). This will be especially challenging for them as the exposure to the sexualized world of trafficking may also make them more liable to sexual exposure and even experimentation when in rehabilitation.[12] Part of their recovery process is not only to process their experience of sexual abuse but also to re-learn healthy ways of relating to both sexes. This is really a training in chastity, which for all is a challenge, but more so when these girls have been victims of gross boundary violations from sex trafficking.

A widely accepted secular view is to encourage young persons with same-sex feelings to "come out." This view however is founded on an erroneous cultural interpretation that all sexual feelings are equally valid and should be promoted and encouraged. It is highly inappropriate when dealing with SSA post-sex trafficking as what we are likely dealing with may be a type of "pseudo-lesbianism" post-trauma. The focus should be on "coming out" of the trauma. There is no apparent literature on how best to rehabilitate a girl with SSA post-sex trafficking. Perhaps the next best thing is to glean what we can from experiences of recovery from SSA in non-trafficked women. Janelle Hallman, an experienced therapist, tells us that the rehabilitation of a woman with SSA

> will be a lengthy process in which she reclaims, piece by piece, her heart and soul, which have been housed or deposited in the other woman. She must salvage the threads of her true self and reknit them around new perceptions, impressions and beliefs that arise out of a corrective experience of love, support and acceptance. (Hallman 2008, 114)

With therapy and counseling the girl may be able to come to terms with the trauma experienced. Sexual behavior should be discouraged, with either sex, in the vulnerable stages of recovery. Chastity and re-integration of the person are noble goals for which to live and strive.

Devastating Consequences of Sex Trafficking on Women's Health

Some healthy contact with males may be beneficial in the recovery process; at least to show that some males can show them respect and not all need to be mistrusted. However, care should be taken in exposing these very vulnerable girls to male contact as the Sisters informed me that there is a danger that the girls can easily fall for a male who shows them even the slightest interest and attention.

The task of assisting in the rehabilitation of girls who have been sex trafficked is a challenging and daunting one. These girls bring with them many deep wounds from abuse and trafficking that are not easy to minister to. However, God's grace is not lacking, and I commend the Sisters for their dedication to their arduous, but noble and hopefully rewarding, charism. I enjoyed celebrating that Eucharist on November 1, the Feast of all the Saints. In the Mass, each girl had come dressed as their favorite saint. It was a sight to behold, not only to see victims of sex trafficking, but also to see the next generation of possible saints: Saint Philomena, Saint Maria Goretti, Saint Teresa of Calcutta, and Saint Thérèse of Lisieux in the making.

Notes

1. Some pertinent details such as the name of the congregation will be omitted. The world of sex trafficking is fraught with dangers for the victims and for those who attempt to assist them. The location of the shelter is kept hidden as sex traffickers seek out the girls to re-coerce them back into the life of sex work,

or threaten and attempt to intimidate them from testifying in future court cases against trafficking rings.

2. Health considerations can extend to an appraisal of the victim's medical condition pre-and post-trafficking as well as during the actual experience of being trafficked. For example, trafficking victims may come from a context of impoverishment and may have some degree of malnutrition before being trafficked.

3. The authors are looking at child victims of prostitution.

4. The Christian Medical and Dental Associations (n.d.) have produced some very helpful and informative modules of continuing medical education on human trafficking including those on the physical and mental-health consequences of human trafficking in general (not specifically on sex trafficking although these are implicitly included).

5. In his lecture "The Holy See and the Fight Against Human Trafficking," at Fordham University, Archbishop Bernardito Auza provides a detailed and insightful list of the various endeavors of Pope Francis to combat sex trafficking (Auza 2017).

6. If evidence of injuries needs to be documented, it should be born in mind that the taking of photos should be explained to minimize risk of provoking traumatic memories of any previous forced pornography experience.

7. This suggestion can also apply to priests and religious. Each year, my community, the Verbum Dei

missionaries, offers a one-day module on prostitution and sex trafficking to novices (mostly young religious men and women at the beginning of their vocation). The group of novices numbers around 70, from 20 or so different congregations and various, mainly Asian, nationalities. It is usually a very enriching exchange, especially seeing how each charism can contribute in a specific way to combat these challenging realities.

8. Many countries have laws and provisions to limit the extent of sex trafficking. However, these laws not always implemented. Where the government does not do its part, the Church cannot sit idly by and do nothing. Pope Emeritus Benedict XVI reminded us of this: "As I have had occasion to say, it is not the proper task of the Church to engage in the political work of bringing about the most just society possible; nonetheless she cannot and must not remain on the sidelines in the struggle for justice" (Benedict 2007).

9. Advocacy and outreach programs are undertaken in bars and on the streets to inform the young women about the drop in center and the services offered there including medical assistance.

10. For a deeper understanding of same-sex attraction according to Catholic Church teaching, various documents can be consulted. Suggested reading includes Homosexuality and Hope by the Catholic Medical Association (2000); Same sex attraction: Catholic teaching and pastoral practice by Rev. Fr. John F. Harvey (2007); "Chastity and homosexuality: Combating the scourge of HIV and AIDS" (McTavish,

2014a); as well as "Spiritual accompaniment of persons with same-sex attraction" (McTavish, 2015) in the Linacre Quarterly special issue on same-sex attraction (Winter 2015).

11. There is literature readily available on sex trafficking of LGBT individuals (see "Sex Trafficking of LGBT Individuals" by Martinez and Kelle 2003, for example).

12. There are some cases of these girls also engaging in inappropriate behavior with other young males. This is understandable, although not advisable, as the girls' concepts of healthy boundaries has been damaged by the experience of sex trafficking making it difficult for them to engage in healthy, non-sexual relationships with others.

References

Auza, Bernardito. 2017. The Holy See and the fight against human trafficking. Inaugural lecture of the Casamarca Foundation Chair in Migration and Globalization at Fordham University, Flom Auditorium, Walsh Library, Fordham University, Bronx, New York, February 23.

Benedict XVI, Pope. 2007. *Sacramentum Caritatis.*

Catechism of the Catholic Church. 1997. 2nd ed. Vatican City: Libreria Editrice Vaticana.

Catholic Medical Association. 2000. *Homosexuality and Hope*. Needham, MA: Catholic Medical Association.

Chiovaro, Francesco. 2003. A Life of Blessed Gennaro Maria Sarnelli. Translated by J. Robert Fenili. Liguori, MO: Liguori Publications.

Christian Medical and Dental Associations. n.d. Human trafficking continuing education modules.

Farley, Melissa. 2004. "Bad for the body, bad for the heart": Prostitution harms women even if legalized or decriminalized. Violence Against Women 10, n. 10: 1087-1125.

Francis, Pope. 2013a. *Evangelii Gaudium*.

Francis, Pope. 2013b. *Urbi et Orbe message*. March 31.

Francis, Pope. 2016. Greeting of his holiness Pope Francis to the second European Assembly of RENATE (Religious in Europe Networking Against Trafficking and Exploitation). November 7.

Hallman, Janelle. 2008. *The Heart of Female Same-Sex Attraction: A Comprehensive Counseling Resource*. Downers Grove, IL: InterVarsity.

Harvey, J. F. 2007. *Same Sex Attraction: Catholic Teaching and Pastoral Practice*. New Haven, CT: Knights of Columbus.

International Organization for Migration (IOM), the Gender Violence and Health Centre of the London School for Hygiene and Tropical Medicine, and the

UN Global Initiative to Fight Trafficking in Persons. 2009. *Caring for Trafficked Persons: Guidance for Health Providers.* Edited by Cathy Zimmerman and Rosilyne Borland. Geneva: International Organization for Migration.

Lederer, Laura J., and Christopher A. Wetzel. 2014. The health consequences of sex trafficking and their implications for identifying victims in healthcare facilities. *Annals of Health Law* 23, n. 1 (Winter): 61-91.

Martinez, Omar, and Guadalupe Kelle. 2013. Sex trafficking of LGBT individuals - A call for service provision, research, and action. *International Law News* 42, n. 4: 21-24.

McTavish, James. 2014a. Chastity and homosexuality: Combating the scourge of HIV and AIDS. *National Catholic Bioethics Quarterly* 14, n. 4: 637-45.

McTavish, James. 2014b. Female same sex attraction. *Ethics and Medics* 39, n. 5: 3-4.

McTavish, James. 2015. Spiritual accompaniment of persons with same-sex attraction. *The Linacre Quarterly* 82, n. 4: 1-9.

National Human Trafficking Resource Center. 2016. *Identifying victims of human trafficking: What to look for in a healthcare setting.*

Rey-Mermet, Théodule. 1998. *Moral choices: The Moral Theology of Saint Alphonsus Liguori.* Translated by Paul Laverdure. Liguori, MO: Liguori Publications.

Devastating Consequences of Sex Trafficking on Women's Health

U.S. Department of State. 2016. *Trafficking in persons report*.

Vatican Council II. 1965. *Gaudium et Spes*.

Willis, Brian M., and Barry S. Levy. 2002. Child prostitution: Global health burden, research needs, and interventions. *Lancet*, 359: 1417-22.

MINISTERS OF LIFE:
A CALL TO MISSION FOR HEALTHCARE WORKERS

Summary

In its new charter, the Vatican calls on healthcare workers to be ministers of life. This is a challenging task and a most noble mission. The mission field itself is the vast, complex and mysterious field of suffering (Pope John Paul II). For Catholic healthcare professionals, it is not so much to have a mission, but to be a mission on this earth, as Pope Francis often reminds us. The daily mission needs to be nourished by a commensurate spirituality. Each deed can be offered to the Lord as part of our response. Healthcare professionals may feel called to specific mission fields too, such as working to reduce the culture of gun violence or to promote the culture of life. The ongoing formation of conscience is a vital prerequisite, so we can continually respond to the novel ethical challenges that progress in technology and medicine inevitably bring. May we each respond enthusiastically to the call to mission: "Here I am Lord, send me!" (Isaiah 6:8).

In its new charter for healthcare workers, the Vatican calls on healthcare workers to be "ministers of life" (Pontifical Council for Pastoral Assistance to Health Care Workers 2017). This is a beautiful title, a noble vocation and a worthwhile dedication - to minister life to the world of today. This is the mission

Ministers of Life: A Call to Mission for Healthcare Workers

of a Catholic healthcare worker - to give life to the world of today. The Church recognizes that to serve the sick is *already* a great mission. Jesus, the divine healer, announced "I have come to give life, life in all its fullness" (John 10:10). This mission of giving, sharing and taking care of life continues today through the life and work of each and every healthcare worker.

In this essay, we will consider 3 inter-connected missionary aspects: the nature of mission, the spirituality of mission and fields of mission.

What Is Mission?

This is the million-dollar question. Often when we think of mission, we would consider having a mission or not. It is interesting that Pope Francis would say you *are* a mission, not that you *have* a mission. In his message for World Mission Sunday in 2019, he wrote "This missionary mandate touches us personally: I am a mission, always; you are a mission, always; every baptized man and woman is a mission" (Francis 2019). He does not use the verb "to have" but "to be." You are a mission on this earth. "Yes, mission impossible" we might be tempted to reply in jest!

St. John Henry Newman (2007) reminds us all,

> Everyone who breathes ... has a mission, has a work. We are not sent into this world for nothing; we are not born at random ... God sees every one of us; He creates every soul, He lodges it in the body, one by one, for a purpose. He needs, He deigns to need, every one of us.

He has an end for each of us... As Christ has His work, we too have ours; as He rejoiced to do His work, we must rejoice in ours also.

No Excuses

Faced with the need to opt for a mission, one trick we might be tempted to employ is a kind of delaying tactic. "I will dedicate more time to the mission when I retire," or "I will give more time and thought to it later, when I am less busy." But who knows how long our life will be? Will we live that long? Later, you might not suddenly gain more interest in mission than you have now. Usually, a dedication or interest takes time to mature and what you sow is what you reap, as St. Paul reminded us (see Galatians 6:7). It is quite amusing to review the varied excuses of different biblical characters, and to discover that really there are no new excuses under the sun.

"I am too young."

Jeremiah complained that he was too young. The Lord told him "Do not say, 'I am too young.' You must go to everyone I send you to and say whatever I command you." (Jeremiah 1:6-7)

"I am too old now."

Abraham was 75 when the Lord called him to leave his land.

"I cannot speak."

That excuse is not so original either. Moses tried it saying, "Pardon your servant, Lord. I have never been eloquent, neither in the past nor since you have spoken to your servant. I am slow of speech and tongue." The Lord replied, "Who gave human beings their mouths? Who makes them deaf or mute? Who gives them sight or makes them blind? Is it not I, the Lord? Now go; I will help you speak and will teach you what to say." (see Exodus 4:10-13)

"I am concerned about my health."

St Timothy, the mission companion of St Paul, had fragile health. One benefit was he was given permission to drink wine. "Stop drinking water only; take a little wine for the good of your stomach and your frequent illnesses." (I Timothy 5:23)

So how great to finally find a willing prophet in the person of Isaiah. May our response be like his. When the Lord said "Whom shall I send? And who will go for us?" Isaiah responds enthusiastically, "Here am I. Send me!" (Isaiah 6:8).

Reconstruct My People

In my life as a medical doctor in the United Kingdom, I pursued my Fellowship in General Surgery. I did not give too much consideration to my calling or mission. If I could survive the on-calls, and get through my exams that would be salvation enough. But with time, seeing difficult cases, accidents, patients dying young, one is faced with inescapable questions about the nature of medical work and inevitably the meaning behind it. I survived my general surgery training which was no small miracle and moved on to my preferred choice - plastic and reconstructive surgery. This was my calling, at least as I understood it at twenty-eight years old. By then, I was in Sydney, Australia, doing research, and working for the Professor of Plastic surgery there. I happened to come across some Missionary Sisters of the Verbum Dei community and was invited to an evening of prayer with the Word of God. That evening, reading the Word of God, "an unknown voice spoke to me" (Psalm 80). This is our Catholic Church teaching - when we pray we speak to God, but when we read the Scriptures God speaks to us as the Second Vatican council (quoting St. Ambrose in the conciliar document "Dei Verbum," the Dogmatic Constitution on Divine Revelation) eloquently reminded us, "we speak to Him when we pray; we hear Him when we read the divine saying" (Vatican Council II 1965, n. 25).

I started to understood the call to give life to the body of Christ. It was Jesus himself, the good Doctor, inviting me to "Reconstruct my people." I was doing that in my specialty, but I felt the call in a deeper way. Perhaps like Peter, the fisherman, being invited to become a fisher of people. Jesus did not change his profession, but asked him to deepen the same call.

I can honestly tell you after more than twenty years in the missionary life, having missioned in many lands, and with various years as a priest, the Lord has been faithful to his call. Through my little life, and the work of my community, I have seen many lives reconstructed and many families rebuilt. I give thanks to our Lord, the divine surgeon, for allowing me to be his assistant in the work of reconstructing his face in the life of so many people.

So now you are asking, "So Fr James what you are telling me is that I have to leave the medical profession and become a nun? Please explain that to my colleagues, never mind my husband and three kids!" Relax! What I am saying is that:

-You do have a mission, a very unique one.

-In doing your God-given mission lies your fulfillment and happiness. Often, there are many misunderstandings about what is mission, and what it is not.

-Your mission needs to be discerned, and that it can change, or perhaps better, evolve.

Spirituality of Mission

Our mission needs to be nourished by a commensurate spirituality. You cannot give what you first don't receive. If in our mission work, we are not suitably inspired, we might just expire. We really need to be contemplatives in action, with a spirituality capable of discovering what is transcendent, the "extraordinary in the ordinary." The updated Vatican charter for Healthcare workers challenges us, remarking, "animated by the Christian spirit and outlook, the health care worker discovers the transcendent dimension peculiar to his profession in its everyday practice. In fact, it surpasses the purely human level of service to the suffering person and takes on the character of Christian witness, and therefore of mission" (Pontifical Council for Pastoral Assistance to Health Care Workers 2017, n. 8). Why is it sometimes we feel overwhelmed by our mission, as if it is just too much and end up asking the Lord if he was not better off calling someone else?

What are some simple ways then to renew and revive our spirituality of mission? Many could be said, and many grand tomes have already been written. Allow me to just share three brief pointers here.

An "only beginning" spirituality.

Once I got a shock after spending some years helping start up a new community in a challenging mission context. I was feeling pretty pleased with myself after all we had worked hard, celebrated the sacraments especially the holy Eucharist, listened to countless confessions, met thousands (literally) of people, guided countless retreats and recollections in Parishes, schools and colleges, given many formations on a variety of pastoral problems and the list of good deeds went on and on. I happened to come across a few lines from *Redemptoris Missio*, an encyclical of Pope John Paul II on mission. I read the opening lines where it said that after 2000 years the mission of the Church ... I paused and imagined what came next ... perhaps "is bearing much fruit" or "has done so much good." Imagine my surprise when I saw what is actually written - after 2000 years the mission of the Church is only just beginning! In his own words,

> The mission of Christ the Redeemer, which is entrusted to the Church, is still very far from

Ministers of Life: A Call to Mission for Healthcare Workers

completion. As the second millennium after Christ's coming draws to an end, an overall view of the human race shows that this mission is still only beginning and that we must commit ourselves wholeheartedly to its service. (John Paul II 1990, n. 1)

Can I invite you from this moment onwards to live an "only beginning" spirituality?

Do small things with love.

The first time I gave a retreat to the Missionaries of Charity, the Sisters of Mother Teresa, I hoped they would be impressed with my deep spirituality and knowledge of their charism. The passage that day for reflection was chapter 25 of Matthew's Gospel, where Christ states, "I was hungry and you gave me something to eat, I was thirsty and you gave me something to drink, I was a stranger and you welcomed me in, I needed clothes and you clothed me, I was sick and you looked after me, I was in prison and you came to visit me ... whatever you did for one of the least of these brothers and sisters of mine, you did it for me" (Matthew 25:35-36). I had heard this teaching was termed by Mother Teresa "the Gospel on five fingers." I just presumed that these were the various scenarios described by Christ and in the middle of my reflection to the Sisters I invited them to fully live out the five tasks - feed the hungry, give a drink to the thirsty, welcome the stranger, cloth the naked, look after the sick, and visit the prisoners. Imagine my horror and slight confusion, counting on my fingers in front of them, and discovering that there are actually six scenarios described, not five. Later one of the Sisters came up to me. "Father that was a lovely reflection. By the way, the 'Gospel on five fingers' is not the various scenarios, but the five-word phrase 'You did it to me!'" You live and learn!

When you attend to the sick, you are attending to Christ himself. Wow! It might be you are visiting a sick patient, taking a call, giving medical advice, prescribing a medicine, or talking with a colleague. How differently we might live these small moments of mission if we could remember those words of our Lord each time, "when I was sick you visited me. Whatever you do to the least of these brothers and sisters of mine, you did it to me." These small tasks/acts/deeds are the bread and butter of our daily mission. They may be small but they add up! M&M's are small but keep eating them and the whole pack is gone. Pope Francis (2020) in his Lenten message for 2021 noted:

> A small amount, if given with love, never ends, but becomes a source of life and happiness. Such was the case with the jar of meal and jug of oil of the widow of Zarephath, who offered a cake of bread to the prophet Elijah (cf. 1 Kings 17:7-16); it was also the case with the loaves blessed, broken and given by Jesus to the disciples to distribute to the crowd (cf. Mk 6:30-44). Such is the case too with our almsgiving, whether small or large, when offered with joy and simplicity.

Ministers of Life: A Call to Mission for Healthcare Workers

The splendid example of many Saints shows us how much progress can be made by persistently doing "small" things with great love. Just look at a twenty-four-year-old religious woman who never left her convent - yes you guessed it, St. Thérèse of Lisieux. She declared "I am a *very little* soul who can only offer *little things* to God" (Thérèse of Lisieux 1957, 146). The Patroness of Catholic missions offered the bread and butter of her daily life, like restraining her irritation at the fidgeting sister in the community, or bearing it patiently when washing handkerchiefs and the other sister inadvertently was splashing her with dirty water. "Great deeds are forbidden me ... how am I to show my love? ... The only way I can prove my love is by scattering flowers and these flowers are every little sacrifice, every glance and word, and the doing of the least actions for love" (Thérèse of Lisieux 1957, 163).

Do it for the Lord

One guiding principle which helps make our work our mission is whatever you do, do it for the Lord. This was the advice of St. Paul to the Colossians, "Whatever you do, work at it with all your heart, as working for the Lord" (Colossians 3:23). It reminds me of the story of the three people laying bricks. The first, looking lethargic and bored, seemed to be laying about one brick an hour. When they were asked why they were working the first replied "Because someone told me to." The second person, who was only marginally faster, and still with a long face replied, "Because they will pay me." The third person was remarkable. She was laying more bricks than the two others combined, was smiling and whistling away full of joy. "How come you are so motivated just to be laying bricks?" they asked her. "I am not simply laying bricks," she explained. "Actually, I am building a wall, and it will be the main wall of a cathedral, and in this house of worship, many will come to know God."

It all depends on our motivation and who we are doing it for! Our whole day, with all the events, ups and downs, joys and sorrows, can be offered to the Lord. St. John Chrysostom (1860) encourages us,

> Our spirit should be quick to reach out toward God not only when it is engaged in meditation; at other times also, when it is carrying out its duties, caring for the needy, performing works of charity, giving generously in the service of others, our spirit should long for God, and call him to mind, so that these works may be seasoned with the salt of God's love, and so make a palatable offering to the Lord of the universe. (PG 64, 462-3)

And St. Paul underlines once more "whatever you do, whether in word or deed, do it all in the name of the Lord Jesus, giving thanks to God the Father through him" (Colossians 3:17).

Mission Fields

Each one of us needs a mission field. While it is true that the daily life setting is a rich source, and summit, for mission, nonetheless we should remain attentive to where else the Lord may be calling us. Let us consider

Ministers of Life: A Call to Mission for Healthcare Workers

the parable of the hidden treasure to explore further potential mission fields: "The kingdom of heaven is like treasure hidden in a field. When a man found it, he hid it again, and then in his joy went and sold all he had and bought that field" (Matthew 13:44). Have you found your mission field yet?

In the United Kingdom, there was an amazing find of Anglo-Saxon treasure at the site which came to be known as "Sutton Hoo" around 100 miles from London. A buried ship was found, along with an incredible collection of treasure including weapons, a helmet, and gold jewelry. The site had previously been visited by robbers, but they did not find the treasure as they had been digging in the wrong place! Lord, teach us how to dig in the right place. To be able to find the treasure in our very work as Catholic Healthcare workers.

Where is the field? In a fascinating statement, John Paul II (1989) explained the specific mission field of healthcare workers: "Your vocation is one which commits you to the noble mission of service to people in the vast, complex and mysterious field of suffering" (n. 2). How to discern one's mission field? In his apostolic exhortation on the call to holiness in the contemporary world, Pope Francis (2018a) advises:

> You too need to see the entirety of your life as a mission. Try to do so by listening to God in prayer and recognizing the signs that he gives you. Always ask the Spirit what Jesus expects from you at every moment of your life and in

every decision you must make, so as to discern its place in the mission you have received. Allow the Spirit to forge in you the personal mystery that can reflect Jesus Christ in today's world. (n. 23)

There are various mission fields for healthcare workers. I will simply cite three examples which can be lived as mission fields.

No to Gun Violence

The gun homicide rate in the United States is 25.2 times higher than that of other high-income countries (Crebs, Sauaia, and Moore 2016, 847). Some doctors feel called to do something about this tragically high figure and make it part of their mission to change the culture of violence around them. Even if many have become accustomed to it as "normal," St. Paul exhorts us, "do not conform to the standards of this world, but allow your mind to be transformed" (see Romans 12:2). Conversion is needed. Ministers of life need to fight for what is right, even if it means going against the grain. "God, who loves life, has entrusted it to the hands of man so that he might be its impassioned guardian. In order to respond to this ennobling vocation, it is necessary to have the willingness to undergo an interior conversion, to purify one's heart, and to find a new outlook" (Pontifical Council for Pastoral Assistance to Health Care Workers 2017, Conclusion).

In their editorial in the *Journal of Trauma and Acute Care Surgery*, Crebs et al. underline that "reduction of gun-related violence entails the need for wholesale cultural change. Science and medicine are excellent instigators of progress, and calls for expanded research into reducing gun violence are mounting in the research community" (Crebs, Sauaia, and Moore 2016, 848). Malina et al., writing in the *New England Journal of Medicine*, echo this call for cultural change.

> Previous commentators including Hemenway and Miller have listed among the steps toward reducing gun violence "changing social norms." Given that it requires "deep cultural changes," however, that is far easier said than done - it is, as Wintemute has argued, "the work of generations." But it is work that we need to begin. If we never address the underlying beliefs that sustain this guns-everywhere extremism, we will not be able to diminish its power." (Malina et al. 2016, 176)

To bring certain wayward aspects of the surrounding culture more into line with Gospel values is a challenging but worthwhile mission.

Yes to the Ongoing Formation of Conscience

In the healthcare professions, so much attention is rightly given to medical updating, but ethical updating needs to keep abreast too. More and more nowadays, medical staff are confronted with medico-ethical issues such as abortion, in vitro fertilization, gender issues, and end of life care to name a few. As John Paul II remarked

> the development of science and technology, this splendid testimony of the human capacity for understanding and for perseverance, does not free humanity from the obligation to ask the ultimate religious questions. Rather, it spurs us on to face the most painful and decisive of struggles, those of the heart and of the moral conscience (John Paul II 1993, n. 1).

There is an urgent need to continually update the conscience. Indeed, the education of the conscience is a lifelong task (Catechism of the Catholic Church 1997, n. 1784).

How to form the conscience? The most recent Synod of Bishops (2018) gives solid advice:

> To reach the deepest dimension of conscience, according to the Christian vision, it is important to cultivate the interiority that thrives on periods of silence, on prayerful, attentive contemplation of the Word, on the sustenance gained from the sacraments and from Church teaching. Moreover we need to develop the habit of doing good, which we review in our examination of conscience: an exercise which is not just about identifying sins, but includes recognizing God's work in our daily lives, in the events of our history and our cultures, in the witness of so many other men and women who went before us or who accompany us with their wisdom. All this helps us to grow in the virtue of prudence, giving an overall direction to our

Ministers of Life: A Call to Mission for Healthcare Workers

life through concrete choices, in the serene awareness of our gifts and limitations. (Synod of Bishops 2018, n. 108)

In a particular way, the Catholic healthcare worker would do well to familiarize him or herself with the Church teaching (Magisterium) on the relevant bioethical issues at hand, especially the ones they deal with in their clinical practice or that are particularly relevant for their cultural context. The Magisterium of the Church has that specific task - to help form the conscience of the believer in these areas. The formation of conscience is indeed an essential part of the mission of the Church, and this is explicitly stated in her teachings. "The intervention of the magisterium falls within its mission of contributing to the formation of conscience" (Congregation for the Doctrine of the Faith 2008, n. 10). The Vatican charter for healthcare workers also underlines that the Church contributes to the formation of conscience as healthcare workers "cannot be left alone and burdened by unbearable responsibilities when confronted with ever more complex and problematic clinical cases, which are made so by the biotechnological possibilities, many of them still in the experimental phase that are available to medicine today, and by the social-health care relevance of particular questions" (Pontifical Council for Pastoral Assistance to Health Care Workers 2017, n. 6).

In this specific area of conscience formation for healthcare workers, the Vatican charter further remarks:

> Advances in medicine and the constant appearance of new moral questions, therefore, require on the part of the health care worker a serious preparation and ongoing formation in order to maintain the necessary professional competence. To this end it is desirable that all health care workers be suitably trained and that those responsible for their professional formation endeavor to establish professorial chairs and courses in bioethics. Furthermore, in the principal hospital centers, the establishment of ethics committees for medical practice and clinical ethics services should be promoted. (Pontifical Council for Pastoral Assistance to Health Care Workers 2017, n. 5)

No to the Death Penalty

Being ministers for life, we need to say yes to life, and no to all that attacks it. For centuries, the Church for various reasons permitted the death penalty. But in recent years, she has seen that the death penalty is inadmissible. In its letter to the Bishops, the Congregation for the Doctrine of the Faith explained this development in Church teaching.

> If, in fact, the political and social situation of the past made the death penalty an acceptable means for the protection of the common good, today the increasing understanding that the dignity of a person is not lost even after committing the most serious crimes, the deepened understanding of the significance of

penal sanctions applied by the State, and the development of more efficacious detention systems that guarantee the due protection of citizens have given rise to a new awareness that recognizes the inadmissibility of the death penalty and, therefore, calling for its abolition. (Congregation for the Doctrine of the Faith 2018, n. 2)

Thus, Pope Francis invoked a revision (stated below in full) of number 2267 of the *Catechism of the Catholic Church*. It is a most important updating to Catholic teaching:

The death penalty

> 2267. Recourse to the death penalty on the part of legitimate authority, following a fair trial, was long considered an appropriate response to the gravity of certain crimes and an acceptable, albeit extreme, means of safeguarding the common good.
>
> Today, however, there is an increasing awareness that the dignity of the person is not lost even after the commission of very serious crimes. In addition, a new understanding has emerged of the significance of penal sanctions imposed by the state. Lastly, more effective systems of detention have been developed, which ensure the due protection of citizens but, at the same time, do not definitively deprive the guilty of the possibility of redemption.

> Consequently, the Church teaches, in the light of the Gospel, that "the death penalty is inadmissible because it is an attack on the inviolability and dignity of the person", and she works with determination for its abolition worldwide (Holy See Press Office 2018).

Regarding the death penalty, while it is true all people of good will should be concerned, it is also true that Doctors and healthcare workers have a powerful voice in society when it comes to issues that directly touch human life. Let us each do our little bit to ensure this updated teaching gets diffused "to the ends of the earth" (Acts 1:8).

Evolving Mission Fields

It is also true that mission fields can change or should we say evolve. Look at the life of Jesus and the gradual revelation of his mission field. When he met the Syrophoenician woman, our good Lord announced his mission field was only to the lost sheep of the house of Israel. He would not give the bread of his teaching to nourish the pagans. Such was his understanding when he came upon the Syrophoenician woman. When she pleaded for the life of her daughter, Jesus said to her, "It is not good to take the children's bread and throw it to the dogs." In a flash she retorted, "Yes, Lord; but please help, for even the puppies feed on the crumbs that fall from their masters' table" (see Matthew 15:21-28). *Touché!* St Matthew shares to us the effect of her words: "Then Jesus said to her, 'O woman, your faith is great; it shall be done for you as you desire'. And her daughter was healed at once." Later the risen Lord would announce the universal mission mandate to all his followers "Go to all nations" (see Matthew 28:19).

The onset of the coronavirus pandemic has brought upon us a necessary rethink of our mission work. In the community I am in, Verbum Dei, we have had to reconsider the scope and nature of our specific mission while still being faithful to our charism. This requires what is known as "creative fidelity" (John Paul II 1996, n. 37). For example, in our mission apostolate prior to the pandemic, we would gather in groups to pray and reflect on the Word of God. Since the pandemic began, this has not been possible. The presential gatherings diminished or stop but the mission goes on, on line. Now instead of the usual "School of the Word" (SOW) it became a "Zoom of the Word" (ZOW). Whereas before there were certain limitations on participation (before you had to live in travelling distance of the SOW) but now the ZOW participation can be intercontinental. How wonderful an opportunity the pandemic presents! Imagine, those Catholic Healthcare workers, who currently may be inhibited from teaching in person, they could fairly easily go on line and share their wisdom and learnings in many resource-poor settings of the developing world. As Pope Francis noted, "The ends of the earth, ... nowadays are quite relative and always easily "navigable." The digital world - the social networks that are so pervasive and readily available - dissolves borders, eliminates distances, and reduces differences" (Francis 2018b). Let us ask the same Spirit that guided

Jesus to lead us to a deeper understanding of our evolving mission fields, thus contributing to the global mission of the Church. Of course, this begins right where we are, but it does not stop there.

Global Mission

A sound starting point is the mission right where we are. We can "grow where we are planted" (but fully available to also be uprooted and transplanted somewhere farther by the Lord!) In this regard, I like so much the words of Dr. Marie-Alberte Boursiquot (2017), a past President of the Catholic Medical Association (USA):

> Please be mindful of your duty both individually and collectively (i.e. guilds) to evangelize our culture. There are various ways of doing this such as taking the opportunity to speak in the public square, working with your local catholic conference, sponsoring guild events which serve to educate the public and guild members on matters pertaining to healthcare. Be encouraged to reach out to your Archbishop/Bishop in offering to be a resource on matters pertaining to the ethical delivery of healthcare in America.

Each of us is called to do our part to contribute to the global mission of the Church. To reach the four corners of the earth is much easier today. In previous centuries, a hazardous sea journey of many months, even years was required. Nowadays, with one click you can be connected globally. How great if more can bring their medical knowledge and expertise to remoter places. We can pray for a new missionary "exodus," where doctors and healthcare professionals could respond to a missionary call to share their sound Catholic medical ethical teaching to many who are just waiting for the scraps of teaching that fall from the table (see Matthew 15:27). Paraphrasing our friend St. Paul (and inserting the word "teach" where he puts "preach") he says "And how can they hear without someone to teach? And how can people teach unless they are sent? As it is written, "How beautiful are the feet of those who bring the good news" of Catholic medical ethics! (see Rom 10:14-15).

If you don't have a mission, then get one. If we are not sure which mission, then fine, just ask the Lord. There is plenty of work - the harvest is large and the laborers are few (Matthew 9:37). Each one of us is personally invited to do our part, to not just bring light to the world, but bring it to your world because no one else can do that. For that specific mission you are irreplaceable! Once again, Pope Francis animates us, "the new evangelization calls for personal involvement on the part of each of the baptized. So what are we waiting for?" (Francis, 2013, 120)

We are all involved in the response to God's call, each and every one of us. He shares his Life to us, so we can share it to others. Let us pray for each other, and for the grace to be faithful ministers of Life.

References

Boursiquot Marie-Alberte. 2017. "Letter of the President to CMA Colleagues and Members (January 10)."

Catechism of the Catholic Church. 1997. 2nd ed. Vatican City: Libreria Editrice Vaticana.

Chrysostom, John. 1860. "Homily about Prayer "De Precatione."" In *Patrologia Graeca*, edited by J. P. Migne Paris.

Congregation for the Doctrine of the Faith. 2008. *Dignitas Personae*.

Congregation for the Doctrine of the Faith. 2018. "Letter to the Bishops Regarding the New Revision of Number 2267 of the *Catechism of the Catholic Church* on the Death Penalty." September 2.

Crebs, J. L., A. Sauaia, and E. E. Moore. 2016. "Gun Violence in the United States: A Call to Action." *Journal of Trauma and Acute Care Surgery* 80, n. 6: 847-48.

Francis, Pope. 2013. *Evangelii Gaudium*.

Francis, Pope. 2018a. *Gaudete et Exsultate*. The Call to Holiness in the Contemporary World.

Francis, Pope. 2018b. "Together with Young People, Let Us Bring the Gospel to All." Message of His Holiness Pope Francis for World Mission Sunday, May 20.

Francis, Pope. 2019. "Baptized and Sent: The Church of Christ on Mission in the World." Message of His Holiness Pope Francis for World Mission Sunday, June 9.

Francis, Pope. 2020. "'Behold, we are going up to Jerusalem'" (Mt 20:18). Lent: a Time for Renewing Faith, Hope and Love." Message of the Holy Father Francis for Lent 2021.

Holy See Press Office. 2018. "New Revision of Number 2267 of the *Catechism of the Catholic Church* on the Death Penalty - Rescriptum 'ex Audentia SS.mi'."

John Paul, Pope, II. 1989. To Representatives of the Italian Catholic Physicians [March 4], n. 2: *Insegnamenti* XII/1.

John Paul, Pope, II. 1990. *Redemptoris Missio*.

John Paul, Pope, II. 1993. *Veritatis Splendor*.

John Paul, Pope, II. 1996. *Vita Consecrata*.

Malina, Debra, Stephen Morrissey, Edward W. Campion, Mary Beth Hamel, and Jeffrey M. Drazen. 2016. "Rooting Out Gun Violence." *New England Journal of Medicine* 374, n. 2: 175-76.

Newman, John Henry. 2007. "Discourse 6. God's Will the End of Life."

Pontifical Council for Pastoral Assistance to Health Care Workers. 2017. *New Charter for Health Care*

Workers. National Catholic Bioethics Center, Philadelphia.

Synod of Bishops. 2018. *Final Document of the Synod of Bishops on Young People, Faith and Vocational Discernment.*

Thérèse of Lisieux. 1957. *The Autobiography of Saint Thérèse of Lisieux - The Story of a Soul*. Translated by John Beevers. New York: Random House.

Vatican Council II. 1965. *Dei Verbum*.

JESUS THE DIVINE PHYSICIAN

Recommendations (in full)

In *Jesus the Divine Physician*, Fr. James McTavish has compiled 14 outstanding award-winning essays in medical ethics from a faith-based perspective. They address a broad range of urgent and ethically challenging questions arising in health care that Catholic and other faith-based healthcare professionals need to address in an ethically sound way to continue and advance the healing and saving mission of Christ in health care today.

Half of the essays focus on the need among health care professionals to develop and sustain a faith-based ethos and how such an ethos ought to pervade the person's whole attitude (joyful) and approach to those one serves and to one's co-servants (compassion and concern). The other essays address the full range of the human experience of being mortal. They range from the individual and social dimensions of applying this ethos at the beginning of life to people who are sick, suffering, and dying at the end of life. In all cases, Fr. James shows how faith needs to be informed by sound ethical reasoning and informed by Catholic social teaching.

For each of these often medically and socially complex realities, Fr. James communicates clearly and simply his solid grasp of the medical realities that he often illustrates using memorable and humorous examples from his own experience. This aspect of his essays

Recommendations (in full)

manifests his impressive medical credentials and prior life as a surgeon. He also highlights and clarifies with remarkable nuance the ethical dimensions of faith-based responses to such realities. This aspect of his essays manifests an impressive depth and breadth of understanding and respect for core teachings of the Catholic moral tradition and of old and new thinkers from other traditions (Aristotle). Most fundamentally, in these essays, Fr. James manifests his life-changing commitment to implementing and advancing Jesus' healing and saving mission in health care today by inviting his readers to join him and many others on this world-changing journey. *William F. Sullivan, MD, CCFP, PhD (Philosophy), Professor of Family Medicine, Georgetown University School of Medicine / Joseph P. Kennedy Sr. Chair in Bioethics, Kennedy Institute of Ethics / Senior Scholar, Kennedy Institute of Ethics, Georgetown University / Member, Pellegrino Center for Clinical Bioethics, Georgetown University School of Medicine, Washington, DC, USA / Ordinary Member, Pontifical Academy for Life*

An engaging series of essays on topics of great contemporary interest. His discussions addressing the way that the life of faith impacts the ministry of health care workers and the paramount importance of an intense spiritual life and solid spiritual formation for physicians and nurses are eminently helpful. *Father Tad Pacholczyk, Ph.D., The National Catholic Bioethics Center, Philadelphia, USA*

JESUS THE DIVINE PHYSICIAN

'Jesus, the Divine Physician' is a thoughtful, provocative and impassioned examination of Catholic teaching on medicine and medical ethics. Fr McTavish draws on his personal experience as a doctor and as a missionary, sharing anecdotes that are sometimes amusing, and self-deprecating, other times deeply moving and powerful. He challenges the reader to consider their conscience, their faith and their attitudes to sickness, mortality and brotherly love. He is not afraid to tell unwelcome truths and to give his reader or listener 'indigestion' at times! Readers who are interested in Catholic medical ethics will find much practical wisdom here. *Professor Dominic Wilkinson, Professor of Medical Ethics, University of Oxford*

Should my practice of medicine be different because of my Catholic faith? Well, at least let it be prayerful, professional, and pro-poor!

Fr McTavish brings the light of faith to his medical training and clinical encounters. His habit of thoughtful reflection on his experiences makes these essays worthy of careful reading. They are fruits of a Catholic faith and professional commitment in different clinical settings - an emergency room or an intensive care ward in an affluent country, the tenement home of a poor family in a low-income setting.

Fr McTavish's experience as both physician and surgeon, together with his mastery of theology and ethics, enables him to speak - to teach! - in an

Recommendations (in full)

authoritative and inspiring way of the challenges that healthcare practitioners encounter when, collaborating with patients living in affluence or in poverty, they strive to live up to the highest goal of their profession: making and keeping the patient well. *Dr Bernadette Tobin, Director, Plunkett Centre for Ethics, Australian Catholic University @ St Vincent's Public Hospital Sydney.*

Father James McTavish was a doctor prior to being ordained to the priesthood. He has a wealth of experience in both the medical and priestly fields as shown in this splendid book. It is an excellent spiritual guide for Catholics in healthcare. *Dr Pravin Thevathasan, Consultant Psychiatrist, Editor, Catholic Medical Quarterly, UK*

Fr. James McTavish brings his extensive experience as a physician, a theologian, and a pastor working for many years in the Philippines and other countries to reflect upon the vocational call of health care workers and pressing moral issues in health care. Attentive readers will find this book equally inspiring, challenging, and thought-provoking. *Jason T. Eberl, Ph.D., Professor of Health Care Ethics and Philosophy & Director, Albert Gnaegi Center for Health Care Ethics, Saint Louis University, Missouri, USA*

I have the honor of sharing with Father James the mission in the same Verbum Dei Missionary family. Every day I continue learning much from his testimony and dedication. I am sure that for those of us dedicated to evangelization, reading his essays motivates us to respond with seriousness and dedication to the questions that we frequently find ourselves confronted by in different areas of our missionary work.

'Jesus, the Divine Physician' is a book that offers great insights to help men and women of good will who work in the health area, opening up possibilities for reflection and guidance for an assertive response to human suffering and pain. *Alfonso Martinez Luna, General responsible (with his wife Adriana) of the Verbum Dei Missionary Couples, Bachelor of Theology and Medical Doctor*

This collection of essays delves deeply into the person and presence of Jesus the Healer, living and breathing in the minds, hearts and hands of healthcare workers in the world of today. As a neonatologist in a national university hospital here in the Philippines, I work with teams of young physicians, as we give the best of our abilities to help families who are burdened with the birth of a premature baby or a newborn who is very sick or afflicted with severe congenital anomalies.

The principles and insights shared by Fr. James in this book serve as very practical signposts in navigating the difficult and evolving ethical issues we face daily in the NICU (neonatal intensive care unit), especially in the setting of limited and unequal distribution of resources. I highly recommend this book as a reference and

Recommendations (in full)

treasure for anyone called to care for the sick, who desire a better life for others, by giving away our own as "ministers of life." *Dr. Resti Ma. M. Bautista, Neonatologist*

Fr James McTavish's reflections are incredibly accessible, and highlight Catholic practical wisdom from the heart of Jesus in the midst of the Church's mission. Ethicists, doctors and nurses, and anyone wrestling with life and death issues of any kind will learn much, feel inspired and be challenged to step up to the need at hand. As he writes, if you don't have a mission, find one. Highly recommended! *Dr Nigel Zimmerman, Adjunct Senior Lecturer, University of Notre Dame Australia*

About the author

Fr James is a Catholic missionary priest, a member of the Verbum Dei missionaries. Originally from Scotland he spent over 18 years assigned in the Philippines, and has participated in the mission in various countries such as Italy, Mexico, Japan, Malaysia, England, Australia, Taiwan, Spain, and Cameroon.

He studied Medicine at Cambridge University, England and qualified as a Medical Doctor. He gained his Fellowship in General Surgery from the Royal College of Surgeons in Edinburgh (FRCSEd) before working as a surgeon and specializing in Plastics and Reconstruction.

He then heard the call of the Lord to heal the Body of Christ through evangelization - "Give me life by your Word" (Psalm 119). He studied Moral Theology and Bioethics in Rome graduating *Summa Cum Laude* in both before teaching courses in Moral theology and Bioethics at various medical and theological schools.

He has published over 75 articles on medical ethics, sexual ethics and bioethics in local and international journals. He has also written various books on Spirituality, on the Verbum Dei founder Fr Jaime Bonet, FMVD, and also on Moral theology topics.

Fr James McTavish, FMVD, FRCSEd, STL, MA (Bioethics)

"Not to us, Lord, not to us but to your name give glory because of your faithfulness and love"
(Psalm 115:1)

Books by same author

Sharper than a Sword

Choose Life

Matters of the Heart

Guidelines regarding End-of-Life issues

A Heart on Fire (co-authored)

Go and Make Disciples (co-authored)

Decision making in Neonatal End-of-Life Scenarios

A Time of Mercy

Form Apostles

A Life of Prayer

"By this is my Father glorified, that you bear much fruit" (John 15:8)

"Your word, Lord, heals all things" (Wisdom 16:22)

Printed in Great Britain
by Amazon